Healing Your Family Tree is a delightful, easy-to-read book tnat analyzes the causes of crippling family habits and proposes models for improvement. Not only will it help members of dysfunctional families, the book will equip counselors, psychologists, and others dealing with family issues to identify harmful behavior patterns and develop possible remedies.

BERNADINE CUROE, SVM
LICENSED MENTAL HEALTH COUNSELOR, LORAS COLLEGE, DUBUQUE, IOWA

The richness of this book comes from Beverly Hubble Tauke's experiences with a diverse cross-section of people and cultures, including the men and women at Gospel Rescue Mission. The blending of storytelling and practical applications makes *Healing Your Family Tree* a user-friendly book for caregivers as well as those in search of personal growth.

JUDY ASHBURN, MEd, LPC, CAC
DIRECTOR OF WOMEN'S MINISTRY, GOSPEL RESCUE MINISTRIES, WASHINGTON, D.C.

The novelist William Faulkner once wrote: "The past is not dead; it is not even past." With insight, clarity, and sensitivity, Bev Tauke chronicles the truth of that statement. Using personal, contemporary, historic, and biblical examples, she shows how conscious and courageous decisions and actions can alter the predictable consequences born out of dysfunctional family life.

MARK PETERSBURG
SENIOR PASTOR, KNOLLWOOD COMMUNITY CHURCH, BURKE, VIRGINIA

Beverly Hubble Tauke is a gifted and skilled therapist who brings to her work a passion for helping people understand themselves in the context of their families. *Healing Your Family Tree* is filled with the wisdom and insight Bev has gleaned from her life and her work with people who are hurting.

CHRISTINE S. CONWAY, PhD; JEFFREY S. BERRYHILL, PhD
COFOUNDERS, CORNERSTONE FAMILY COUNSELING, FAIRFAX, VIRGINIA

I have greatly benefited from Bev Tauke's extraordinary insight and loving counsel as it relates to God's mercy and the redemption of families. She has made a tremendous difference in my life and I am sure that lives will be changed forever by *Healing Your Family Tree.*

CINDI WILLIAMS
FORMER CHIEF OF STAFF TO ELIZABETH DOLE, CURRENT WOMEN'S RIGHTS ADVOCATE, WASHINGTON, D.C.

If read with openness, trust, and faith, *Healing Your Family Tree* provides a near guarantee that life will be better. Within these pages are reflections and real-life stories that will give those whose past makes it difficult to move forward the power to change.

REV. RICHARD B. MARTIN
PASTOR, CHURCH OF THE NATIVITY, BURKE, VIRGINIA

This author wisely understands that a family is an interconnected system with each member playing some role, either contributing toward family healing or furthering the brokenness. Here is practical insight on how to be an agent of healing, first for one's self and then others who are a part of the family tree. This book explains how by God's grace one can stop the cycle of dysfunction and move toward the wholeness God intended. I found the book to be very helpful in counseling families that are in emotional and spiritual disarray.

DR. ERWIN LUTZER
THE MOODY CHURCH, CHICAGO

For anyone who wants to work on their family issues, this is a must-read book. Bev is a masterful communicator, poignantly weaving biblical truth with behavioral truth in a spirit of mercy and grace. And the best part is she lives what she teaches. This approach could save some people years of therapy.

DAWN ZIMMERMAN, LPC, DIRECTOR
THE COUNSELING CENTER AT MCLEAN BIBLE CHURCH, VIRGINIA

Beverly Tauke has penned a remarkably helpful book, which has become a true lifesaver for many people. Not only is it a helpful personal resource, I have used this book as a gift to those who now show evidence of healing, and who report that destructive family patterns have been shattered.

JOANNE KEMP, BOARD MEMBER
PRISON FELLOWSHIP INTERNATIONAL

Full of helpful information about meeting the pain of the past and transforming it into abundant living for the future for both clinicians or individuals working on their own families. . . . Tauke wants more for her readers than liberation from negative, life-destroying traits; she wants them to experience healing through a "vibrant, authentic, God-driven, metabolized faith."

THE FAMILY AND MARRIAGE COUNSELING DIRECTORY WEB SITE

Full of inspiring wit and inspiring insight. . . . Tauke dramatically illustrates two principles that flow throughout her book:

- It is possible to identify and correct dysfunctional family habits and break the cycle of pain and unhealthy behavior for future generations.

- Psychological, emotional, spiritual and physical functions are intertwined and interdependent.

THE WITNESS
DUBUQUE, IOWA

Although we are each responsible for our own choices, the truth is that the addictions, fears and dysfunctions in our lives often stretch back to our fathers and mothers and their parents and ancestors. That legacy of brokenness can be ended and replaced with healing and joy, according to Tauke. Her purpose: to show the way to remarkable healing.

CATHOLIC UNIVERSITY OF AMERICA MAGAZINE

Healing Your Family Tree

*A Destiny-Changing Journey toward Freedom,
Forgiveness, and Healthier Relationships*

BEVERLY HUBBLE TAUKE

SALT**RIVER**®

AN IMPRINT OF
TYNDALE HOUSE PUBLISHERS, INC.

Visit Tyndale's exciting Web site at www.tyndale.com

TYNDALE and Tyndale's quill logo are registered trademarks of Tyndale House Publishers, Inc.

SaltRiver and the SaltRiver logo are registered trademarks of Tyndale House Publishers, Inc.

Healing Your Family Tree: A Destiny-Changing Journey toward Freedom, Forgiveness, and Healthier Relationships

Copyright © 2004 by Beverly Hubble Tauke. All rights reserved.

Cover photograph of tree copyright © by NeubauBerlin.com. All rights reserved.

Cover photograph of males copyright © by Michel Touraine/Jupiter Images. All rights reserved.

Author photo copyright © 2003 by Mary Beth LaMarche. All rights reserved.

Designed by Beth Sparkman

Previously published in 2004 as *Sins of the Family* by Tyndale House Publishers, Inc., under ISBN 0-8423-8697-1.

Unless otherwise indicated, all Scripture quotations are taken from the *Holy Bible,* New International Version®. NIV®. Copyright © 1973, 1978, 1984 by International Bible Society. Used by permission of Zondervan. All rights reserved.

Scripture quotations marked KJV are taken from the *Holy Bible,* King James Version.

Scripture quotations marked NLT are taken from the *Holy Bible,* New Living Translation, copyright © 1996, 2004. Used by permission of Tyndale House Publishers, Inc., Carol Stream, Illinois 60188. All rights reserved.

Library of Congress Cataloging-in-Publication Data

Tauke, Beverly Hubble.
  [Sins of the family]
  Healing your family tree : a destiny-changing journey toward freedom, forgiveness, and healthier relationships / Beverly Hubble Tauke.
      p. cm.
  Originally published: Sins of the family. Wheaton, Ill. : SaltRiver, c2004.
  Includes bibliographical references.
  ISBN-13: 978-1-4143-1175-3 (sc)
  ISBN-10: 1-4143-1175-3 (sc)
  1. Family—Religious life. I. Title.
  BV4526.3.T38 2004
  248.4—dc22   2006036464

Printed in the United States of America

12   11   10   09   08   07
7   6   5   4   3   2   1

To my love, joy, and refuge,

Tom,

and to the delights of my life,

Joseph and Elizabeth

SaltRiver Books are a bit like saltwater: Buoyant. Sometimes stinging. A mixture of sweet and bitter, just like real life. Intelligent, thoughtful, and finely crafted—but not pretentious, condescending, or out of reach. They take on real life from a Christian perspective. Look for SaltRiver Books, an imprint of Tyndale House Publishers, everywhere Christian books are sold.

SALTRIVER®

Intelligent. Thought-provoking. Authentic.

www.saltriverbooks.com

CONTENTS

ACKNOWLEDGMENTS

Writing a book, it seems to me, has great similarities to bringing a new life into the world. There are many months of percolating in the system, with a gestation period in this case more similar to an elephant's than a human's. After a great deal of labor, voilà! There it is.

There was even an army of midwives in this process, often working in shifts.

First, my brother-in-law, Jean La Marche, architecture professor at the University of New York, Buffalo, expressed interest in seeing materials from my multigenerational family workshops. At that same time, I was plowing through a series with the homeless men and women in a life-transforming, yearlong residency program at Gospel Rescue Ministries, almost in the shadow of the U.S. Capitol. Each week I summarized the homeless workshop material to ship off for Jean's perusal.

Next my friend Cindi Williams, whose brilliant political

mind is currently based at the White House, asked to see a copy of the material that had already meandered from a homeless program workshop to academia. Concluding that the material was publishable, Cindi's publicist friend, Jana, offered names of agents particularly suited to this type of manuscript.

Agent Leslie Nunn Reed told me that, in fact, she had heard me speak in Washington many years prior (probably the only agent in the nation in this category), and, yes, she would represent the work.

Lunching with Tyndale House senior acquisitions director Jan Long Harris at a Christian Booksellers' convention, Leslie described the project. Unwittingly, Leslie was describing this work to an editor who (I hate to admit this part) *thirty years ago* was an acquaintance of mine when we both were students. Yes, Leslie was told, if I was willing to do some manuscript surgery, Jan Harris thought Tyndale House would be interested.

Meanwhile, my husband and long-ago newspaper reporter, Tom, provided an early warning system for language oddities or confusing passages. Later in the process his sister, Mary Sue Sova—a graduate of the Iowa Writers' Workshop—contributed her savvy radar to the early warning system, sort of a family pre-editing operation.

Tom's younger sister, Mary Beth (Tauke) La Marche, also an architecture professor at the University of New York, Buffalo, and former publishing-house graphic design artist, was drafted as photographer for a backyard mug shot.

My mother, Catherine, and my sister Charlotte deserve

medals for enduring years of family forensics—my effort to unravel centuries, literally, of clan mysteries.

I am quite sure that from heaven, cherished family patriarch (and my father) Ralph smiles at this process, to which his life and observations contributed great value.

Intrigued by this journey, my Richmond, Virginia, cousins and their families instigated church Family Habits presentations and report eagerness to use this book for another round of collective cogitation. Dialogues with my cousins Lois and Debi, and Steve and his wife, Mary, as well as my late cousin, Jody, enriched the work and inspired me personally, for which I am grateful.

Of the many friends whose input has proven empowering, I particularly celebrate the wisdom and insight of Jan Katz, former dialogue partner during our Washington, D.C., political days and now assistant attorney general in the state of Ohio.

Following my own advice to clients, I have compiled a list several pages long of nonrelative heart-warmers to whom I am indebted for an enriched inner world, gentled life journey, and insight into surrogate power explored in chapters ahead. Far beyond my ability to express, I am especially indebted for boosts from Ray, Ruth, and Terry to the teenage me, triggering chains of events profoundly affecting my life trajectory ever since.

Writing skills honed by my college professors Glenn Arnold and the late Jim Johnson launched my professional life and greatly flavor this work.

Finally, I am awed by courageous clients who have

triumphed over generations of crippling family habits. Their journey to wholeness not only transforms them, but also inevitably changes me for the better.

My hope is that those touched by these stories will, as the legendary phoenix, rise to fly above ashes of despair—better yet, even soar.

Beverly Hubble Tauke
Alexandria, Virginia

INTRODUCTION

Sixty-year-old Madeleine J. first landed in the world of Oliver Sacks, neurologist extraordinaire, in 1980, when she left the home of her doting and protective family to enter St. Benedict's Hospital near New York City.

Although blind from birth and afflicted by cerebral palsy, Madeleine was a spirited, eloquent woman "of exceptional intelligence and literacy," reports Sacks in his best-selling *The Man Who Mistook His Wife for a Hat.*[1]

Mystifying medical experts, Madeleine was also hampered by inexplicably inert hands that she described as "useless godforsaken lumps of dough—they don't even feel part of me."

Perhaps the cause resided not in her body, mused Sacks, but in a family that had "'protected,' 'looked after,' 'babied' [her] since birth," thus preventing the development of mind-hand coordination, or even of tactile intelligence. If objects had never been plopped into her palm or between her fingers, how could blind Madeleine internalize any concept of a fork or a hairbrush or a cup?

Madeleine "had no repertoire of memory, for she had never used her hands—and she felt she *had* no hands—or arms either," reports Sacks.

Suspecting that Madeleine's genetic wiring might kick in if stimulated a bit, Sacks directed the staff to solicit, even provoke, impulsive use of Madeleine's hands. They were to occasionally leave Madeleine's food nearby but not to feed it to her.

Sure enough, one day the hungry Madeleine lost patience and groped around, grasped a bagel, and put it to her mouth. *At that moment, a sixty-year-old cocoon of imposed helplessness ruptured and a vitalized Madeleine emerged.*

When her mind and spirit were "deprogrammed" from disabling data, Madeleine's body was set free. With pent-up appetite to explore the tactile world, Madeleine asked for clay to press and mold. Within a year she became famous locally as the Blind Sculptress of St. Benedict's, producing artwork with "remarkable expressive energy," says Sacks.

Like Madeleine, clients who come to me for counseling bring achy hearts and unhealthy relationships. They are often products of epidemic divorce or homes where their souls—not their hands—were neglected and untrained. Many describe their heart, as Madeleine described her hands, as *feeling* useless, numb, confusing, and, yes, godforsaken.

Just as insight into Madeleine's early home environment proved crucial for her physical liberation, so can a study of your family history unleash new psychological and spiritual freedom. Her story dramatically illustrates two principles flowing through this book:

1. It is possible to identify and correct dysfunctional family habits and break the cycle of pain and unhealthy behavior for future generations.

2. Psychological, emotional, spiritual, and physical functions are intertwined and interdependent. In Madeleine's case, an emotional jolt (frustration) triggered a mental shift (the idea to "grab some food despite these 'useless' hands!"), mobilizing inert limbs and revolutionizing her world. Through Madeleine we can see the transforming power of treating humans as complete mind-body-spirit packages—whether by a doctor, a minister, or a therapist.

   Likewise, mounds of data show that *faith-based principles* are an important part of personal, marital, and family healing. Because of this, faith-energized folks have a proven edge in marital satisfaction, cohesion, and emotional and sexual intimacy.[2]

   But on the flip side, Bible-quoting parents who aim authority at children with demoralizing, heart-pulverizing coldness or rage also should know that their behavior actually *increases* the odds that their children will become social deadweight—sexually promiscuous or psychologically and physically abusive.[3]

The third premise, unrelated to marvelous Madeleine, is this: While coercive, malevolent, or evil behaviors in families are tolerated at great peril, there *are* ways to disengage the power of family villains.

On the following pages, we'll celebrate the numerous courageous souls who have embraced these principles and found great reward. Except in rare cases where permission has been granted to use personal stories, clinical illustrations are composites: a blend of cases with great similarities so as to preserve reality while protecting confidentiality. Thus, except for permission granters, any approximation of private (versus public) personalities is not only coincidental but also consciously avoided.

I often use historic or public figures as examples with my clients and in workshops, and I've included them here in an effort to depersonalize struggles common to us all. Their documented triumphs and tragedies are imbued with powerful credibility.

Adding a personal note, I cite the intuition of my ninety-one-year-old father-in-law, Joe, who concluded that this book project is partly about me. Indeed, it is—as is common among writers—partly autobiographical.

By my calculation, my own family actually launched production of this book in about 1847 when William F. "Billy" Hubble was born. Billy, my great-grandfather, rose among a gifted extended family distinguished by medical doctors, scholars, ministers, and PhDs—including his brilliant distant cousin, astronomer Edwin P. Hubble.

Billy was a gifted horseman and driver of four-horse logging wagons. He was, alas, best known for alcoholism and had serious crashes a century before sobriety checks came into vogue.

"Thank God for *Billy!*" some homeless men have exclaimed in my Washington, D.C., workshops when I've revealed my invisible roots. "*Billy* is why you understand *us!*"

Indeed, he is. Sorrow has flowed for generations from Billy, as family roles, communication, and relationships tend to spread in a contagion from an alcoholic patriarch.

Following a mutually gratifying discussion about Billy's legacy just two days before I wrote this, my eighty-four-year-old mother expressed enthusiasm about this project because "we need concrete help for families" in pain. She *gets* Billy's long reach from the nineteenth into the twenty-first century—an understanding that is part of healing.

Ironically, I am greatly indebted to Billy. His legacy, I believe, resulted in an inexplicable strength and radar within me.

The product of a deeply religious family sprinkled with generations of ministers, I am also grateful that my parents seeded within me a faith in Jesus Christ as Son of God and Savior. Transformed into my own rudder and anchor, this faith, I am convinced, holds the key to a life that has proven remarkably challenging, gratifying, and wonderfully adventurous.

The faith connection also offers an extra safety net when I fall into some of the very self- and family-wounding traps I explore in these pages. I confess happily (as it eliminates the pressure of any illusion or delusion of perfection) that I write as a fellow seeker, not as one who has arrived.

Finally, a few words about a research-proven secret to a vibrant, resilient, happy life, as documented by the Harvard Study of Adult Development: As it turns out, a *good marriage* surpasses other factors as key to personality advantages, stability, and happiness throughout life.[4] This consideration alone is powerful motivation for young or solo members of our families to scrutinize the character and habits of potential partners; for miserably partnered readers to resolve agony and conflict within marriages; and for those who are happily connected to celebrate partners who have proven themselves a safe refuge from the turbulence of life.

My personal, joyful, technicolored proof of the study's point is wrapped up in Thomas Joseph Tauke, father of our two wonderful children, the love of my life, and cherished partner for twenty years.

So, yes, Joe. The book *is* partly my story.

ONE
ALL IN THE FAMILY

Leaving work for the day as a public-relations writer in Chicago, I headed for the subway and home. As I crossed LaSalle Street near the Cabrini Green housing project—notorious for muggings and murder—I was startled by movement toward me from the side.

"Could you help us, please?"

I turned to face two girls who appeared to be about sixteen.

"What do you need?" I inquired.

"Could you point us to a cheap hotel?"

Two years out of college myself, I was barely older than these girls. If they were roaming Chicago streets looking for a cheap hotel, I assumed they were in some sort of trouble. *Runaways,* I thought, noting the sleeping bags in their hands.

I asked them a few questions, mostly stalling for time and for a sense of inner direction. Really, I knew of no cheap lodging in a city that seemed very expensive on my starter-job budget. So what were my options, other than leaving them to manage on their own?

"Well, I don't really know of any cheap hotels, but I could try to help you find one."

Two blondish heads nodded.

"Or," I added slowly, calculating risks, "I could take you home with me. Free."

"Really?" they asked, small smiles creeping up their cheeks.

"Look, it's not much. A tiny little apartment. No extra beds. But you can have dinner and a warm bath. You can stretch those sleeping bags out on the rug. But you'll have to leave with me for work early in the morning."

"Sure," they agreed in obvious delight.

As we settled into our subway seats, I looked at the girls and stated the obvious: "This is risky, you know. I don't know you. You don't know me. So we have to trust each other in a bit of an adventure here."

You're totally nuts! is what I was really saying to myself by then—perhaps quite accurately, I conclude years later. I *was* smart enough, however, to shoot up a few prayers for wisdom and protection.

At any rate, we aimed for the Chicago neighborhood where I rented a minuscule attic apartment from an elderly landlord. I pointed the girls to the claw-foot tub so they could take hot baths while I made dinner—chicken, as I recall, as that was the limit of my culinary expertise.

"So, where are you from?" I inquired as we munched dessert—cookies from a box.

They looked at each other tensely and responded that they came from outside Illinois but that was all they would say.

However, before we all drifted off to sleep in the wee hours of the morning, they did tell me about their families.

Train a child in the way he should go, and when he is old he will not turn from it. PROVERBS 22:6

Joanna had fled brutal beatings from her alcoholic dad. The risk of hitting the road with no money and no place to go had finally been eclipsed by the terror of facing her father after school each day. She was more sad than angry and more determined than scared.

Alcohol was no excuse for Bonnie's father, a teetotaler and Bible-quoting church deacon. She wept as she described the beatings he delivered daily, bruises and bloody gashes left not only on five children but on their mother as well.

"What's this?" I inquired, taking her hand and gently touching marks on her wrist.

She turned her head away, silent. Then quietly she murmured, "I did that last year."

"With what?"

"A razor blade."

Failing to leave her tormentor through death, Bonnie had finally summoned the courage to hit the highway. She predicted that one or more of her siblings would soon follow.

"Bonnie, I'm so sorry," I said quietly. "I'm especially sorry that God has been used as a cover for abuse. If you ever needed him you need him now. Please don't let your Bible-quoting, brutalizing father poison your heart against God."

A very strong faith was by then my rudder for life and had

been much of the motivation for giving brief refuge to these desperate young women. To me, it was blasphemy that a father would claim to speak with the voice of God while brutalizing a precious child entrusted to his care.

True to our agreement, Joanna and Bonnie rose for an early subway ride into the heart of Chicago. I celebrated that my bed-and-breakfast offer had comforted two young girls and turned out well. I also felt fear for them as they headed into the unknown, and sorrow for the violence to their bodies and souls that had led them to take such a risk.

Tears filled three sets of eyes as I rose to exit the subway before their chosen stop. "We're very grateful," said Joanna. Bonnie nodded, reaching out for a big hug.

Months drifted by and I nearly forgot the two young strangers who had shared that evening with me. Then a letter arrived from Bonnie. Mostly she wanted to alert me that her older brother was headed to Chicago. Could he call?

Sure, he could call, I told her, but not for bed and breakfast. My place wasn't coed.

Seventeen-year-old Bryan called soon afterward. He wondered if we could meet for lunch.

We talked over steak and eggs in a low-budget diner near the office where I worked at the time. Bryan's story was similar to Bonnie's. So were the marks on his arm.

"Bryan, I have to ask . . . ," I said, touching the scar on his wrist.

This was a one-plot family. Just as Bonnie had lurched for death as relief from the family sadist, so had Bryan. Also like Bonnie, he was grateful to be alive and determined to be free.

A third sibling, Bobby, also connected with me through phone discussions scattered over the next several years. Unlike Bonnie and Bryan, the younger Bobby stuck it out at home with Dad. Recoiling from family violence, he used humor and appeasement, not suicide attempts, to deflect his father's rage. He also tried desperately to win acceptance by stuffing himself into a mold demanded by his father.

Bobby attended a Christian college and returned to his dad's church as youth pastor. The battering deacon finally had a child he found a bit worthy of himself.

Twenty-five years after that first overnight visit, after a decade of silence, I received a call from Bobby. He found me at a Virginia counseling center where I had been working for several years.

The small talk was brief. "I didn't know who else to call. I have to tell someone," said Bobby from his home two thousand miles away.

"I have time. What's on your mind?" I asked.

"I'm gay," said Bobby.

Silence at my end. I was trying to wrap my mind around disjointed images of fundamentalist youth pastor Bobby and gay Bobby.

But I got it. Immediately. *Of course he called me. He would have instantly become a pariah had he confided in his fundamentalist community.*

Not only was Bobby gay, he was also highly promiscuous. Not with a few favorite sexual companions. With strangers. And not just strangers who attracted him with charm, personality, intelligence, or physical appeal. Bobby hung out in sex clubs where faces were hidden and identities protected, places where actions transpired anonymously between rented booths separated by curtains.

And, yes, he was still a fundamentalist youth pastor. No, he was not attracted to young boys nor had he ever had sexual relations with anyone much younger than himself. Yes, his relationship with his father had improved. In fact, he got along better with his father than did any of his four siblings.

No wonder. The deacon was a Christian-community variation of Romans 1:25 (KJV). He had clearly "changed the truth of God into a lie, and worshipped and served the creature more than the Creator." This father was an idolater who worshipped himself and demanded child sacrifice—the wrenching emotional evisceration of his own children—in his self-centered religion. *Bobby was the one child who agreed to what the idolatry demanded.*

Willing to pay any price in order to win his father's love, Bobby had built his life around a faith of his father's design, but one that could hardly be more alien to his inner world. His religion was merely a concoction of his father's, lacking any independent struggle to know or understand God on his own. *But a relationship with the Creator requires connection between one's soul and God, not between oneself and a god impostor.*

SOUL MURDER

Bobby was an extreme example of many cases that have drifted into the counseling center where I work. As counselors, we strive to combine academic and professional training in mental health with a strong commitment to Christ and to biblical principles. Most of our clients come from a broad range of local churches, usually fundamentalist or evangelical, but often Coptic or Catholic as well. Clients need help with mild to extreme emotional problems. Some ache from the inevitable grief of life—lost jobs, lost loves, marital crises, bereavement, loneliness, guilt, depression, or dull aches persisting from childhood.

> A RELATIONSHIP WITH THE CREATOR REQUIRES CONNECTION BETWEEN ONE'S SOUL AND GOD, NOT BETWEEN ONESELF AND A GOD IMPOSTOR.

Others, like Bobby, are walking wounds. Victims of "soul murder," as graphically described by Morton Schatzman in a book of that title, some seem to be the drifting dead, numb to emotions, to a sense of self, to hope for the future, or to any experience of reliable love—*ever.*

Loveless vs. cherished hearts

Bobby's story is not unique. In fact, his life echoes the tragic outcomes of Harvard's Study of Adult Development, the world's longest prospective study of physical and mental health. The study followed Harvard graduates born about 1920, tracking their physical, emotional, mental, and social well-being for more than sixty years. The study also assessed the childhood environment of each subject, producing categories ranging from "loveless" children at one end of the spectrum to "cherished" children at the opposite extreme.

Despite superior minds and elite academic credentials, the

loveless Harvard men were five times as likely as their cherished counterparts to struggle with mental-health crises, including depression or addiction to alcohol or drugs. The loveless tended to navigate life as loners, isolated from close friendships.[1]

The loveless were also three times as likely as the cherished to die before age seventy-five from unnatural deaths, often self-inflicted by unhealthy behaviors (related to lung cancer, cirrhosis, emphysema, and suicide).

Bobby was no Harvard man, but his physically, emotionally, and spiritually treacherous childhood produced consequences matching the research. His sex addiction, which he at times loathed but used habitually to soothe a barren inner world, reflected various types of emotional trauma much more typical of Harvard's loveless than cherished subjects. So far, Bobby had sustained physical health. But in an age of AIDS, his frequent forays into cavalier, indiscriminate, often unprotected sex put him at the same risk faced by Harvard's loveless research subjects.

Destiny-changing habits

What if Bobby's life had been shaped by a loving rather than a battering environment?

Harvard's remarkable research provides some clues. The study's cherished children seemed to be protected against adult depression, addictions, and other forms of mental crises; from chronic illnesses; and from premature death. By age eighty, the cherished death rate was two-thirds lower than the average for their age group.

Harvard's cherished have lived not just longer lives than the loveless, but lives filled with more relationships and enjoyment. The cherished were five times more likely to play competitive sports, to play games with friends, and to take enjoyable vacations. More so than the loveless, they were able to balance duty and obligation with stress-relieving recreation.

CHERISHED CHILDREN SEEMED TO BE PROTECTED AGAINST ADULT DEPRESSION, ADDICTIONS, AND OTHER FORMS OF MENTAL CRISES; FROM CHRONIC ILLNESSES; AND FROM PREMATURE DEATH.

While the loveless often reported friendless lives, the cherished had formed nurturing relationships and seemed to have been strengthened and energized by such connections.

An intriguing insight emerges here that goes back to the ancient parenting guidance to "train a child in the way he should go, and when he is old he will not turn from it" (Proverbs 22:6). When early training is paired with loving relationships, a child is more likely to thrive throughout life due to stable emotions, secure social connections, and physical well-being.

Sadly, Harvard's cherished children pose a stark contrast to the quiet desperation of Bonnie, Bryan, and Bobby. As I listened to Bobby share his secret, I wondered, *How can such crippled lives be products of "Christian" homes?* It was the same question that had haunted me since college days.

I thought about the many traumatized clients who came to see me each week. Many of these people personally struggled to know God and live by biblical principles, yet seemed to drift through life in personality-shriveling, relationship-crippling, spirit-stifling emotional pain. Where was the abundant life assured by Christ? Surely their tormented journey was *not* the vibrant life the Scriptures promise.

> HARVARD'S CHERISHED HAVE LIVED NOT JUST LONGER LIVES THAN THE LOVELESS, BUT LIVES FILLED WITH MORE RELATIONSHIPS AND ENJOYMENT.

I could see that many of the wounded were suffering directly from sins of the fathers (or mothers), or even the toxic choices of grandparents or great-grandparents. As clients recounted their family history, the evidence clearly mounted, proving that destructive ancestral choices often became habits of life. I could see how these habits then became the environment that shaped the personality and character of the next generation. And children whose personalities were distorted by their parents' destructive habits became a new parent generation, doing what now came naturally: poisoning the family tree.

If the poor apples in each successive batch of children seemed shriveled and bruised—no wonder! Was there hope for them? Could they break this multigenerational crash-and-burn cycle?

As I thought about Bobby and others like him, more questions followed:

- Can the loveless learn to live cherished lives?
- What are the family habits that produce cherished lives in the first place?

- Is it possible to transform personal and family destiny by importing those habits?

Such is the focus of this book.

If there were no hope for healing, I would not remain in the counseling profession.

If I had not experienced my own personal healing, I would not find the hope so compelling.

If a vibrant, authentic, God-driven, metabolized faith were not a major key, I would not be awed at the ability of some spiritually empowered clients to pry light from darkness and wring hope from despair.

And if true stories of tragedy transformed into triumph could not dance through these pages, there would be no book.

TRANSFORMING HABIT
Warm your heart through nurturing relationships.

TWO

WIRED FOR WARMTH

As overwhelming as it may seem when stuck in family pain, it is possible to break the destructive generational patterns of our families. The successful shifts of my own family habits have been welcome confirmation of that (see chapter 9).

Remarkably, some loveless children not only heal, but also evolve into adults with extraordinary capacity to warm and nurture others. How do they *do* this? How are some of the most heart-battered children driven to a greatness beyond themselves—*and what can we learn from them?*

Abraham Lincoln, whose heart became a fortress for millions of oppressed slaves, offers an intriguing example of a person who pried triumph out of multigenerational sorrow.

Abe was shaped by a harsh, isolated existence in Kentucky and Indiana frontier territory. After he lost his mother to death when he was nine, his burdens became greater. According to historian William E. Gienapp, Abe and his twelve-year-old sister, Sarah, assumed the grim duties of adult pioneers and were soon described as "wild—ragged and dirty."

Abraham's father, Thomas, brought a new wife from Kentucky to his crude Indiana cabin, which lacked any proper door or windows and featured a dirt floor and half-finished roof. Sarah Bush Johnstone cleaned up the Lincoln children, mended clothes so they would look "more human," and developed an affection for her stepson greater than her feelings for her own children. "Abe was the best boy I ever saw or ever expect to see," she later reported.

But Abe's stepmother could not thaw the chill between father and son. Illiterate, the father had little use for education. He allowed Abe less than a year of formal instruction and resented his son's love for learning. Thomas sometimes "slash[ed] him for neglecting his work by reading," reported a family friend, adding that Thomas "treated him rather unkind."[1] In contrast, Thomas openly favored his stepson, John, which may have deepened the chasm between father and son.

Why was Thomas so depleted in fathering skills? Perhaps because he himself had been molded by tragedy and loss. His father was killed by Indians in rural Kentucky, and from the age of eight Thomas survived as a wandering laboring boy. His childhood illiteracy, poverty, and rootlessness evolved into a crude environment for his own children.

If *sins* of the fathers can torment third and fourth generations, so, too, do *wounds* of the fathers.

With ambition that amazed childhood friends, Abe Lincoln refused to accept the hopeless life of a victim. He took responsibility for his own growth and development. He educated himself, succeeded as a self-made lawyer, twice won the presidency of a young United States, and ultimately liberated a nation from the tragedy of slavery. In these ways the loveless Lincoln pried triumph from tragedy.

Ironically, the achievements for which Abraham Lincoln is most revered were derived from his troubled father. Thomas Lincoln left a church because he rejected its pro-slavery position, and he lit a passion that later consumed his son. Perhaps early trauma gave Abe eyes to see more clearly the suffering of slaves and ears to hear more acutely the cries of the oppressed. And perhaps Abraham Lincoln channeled the agony of a child's battered heart into the determination necessary to set millions of abused captives free.

How can others wring triumph from family trauma, as did Abraham Lincoln? We can follow the steps of Bonnie, daughter of the battering church deacon. As Bonnie learned, it *is* possible to retrofit the software running our heads, hearts, relationships, and destiny.

REWIRE THE SYSTEM

When Bonnie ran away from home at sixteen, she knew one thing for sure: Romance was not for her. She had learned this lesson well from her family-battering father. *Do not trust men!* So she built walls around her heart to keep them out. Friends warned that if she didn't tear down the barricades, she would never marry. "Fine with me!" was her reply.

In this way she seemed the opposite of her brother Bobby, who rapidly collected a varied assortment of male lovers. But at their core, Bonnie and Bobby faced the same issue. Both were wired with love-starved hearts that produced enormous pain. Bobby tried to anesthetize his grief with frequent doses of intimacy with strangers. But, in reality, true intimacy was impossible with those who didn't even know his soul, much less cherish him. Each desperate encounter was really another failure to find the intimacy he so desired.

Bonnie and Bobby were poster children for current research showing that *human beings are wired for warmth*. While "genetics provide the raw material," reports *Newsweek* in a special child-development edition, *"life molds the spirit and soul"* (emphasis added).[2] We *are* wired for warmth. When we are denied warmth as children, bugs are created in our inner software that impact emotions, judgment, and relationships.

> WE ARE WIRED FOR WARMTH. . . . OUR BRAINS ARE LITERALLY PROGRAMMED BY OUR EARLY EMOTIONAL LIFE.

Research has found that children who are denied connection and affection are at risk emotionally.[3] Our brains are literally programmed by our early emotional life. A caregiver's interaction with a child engineers most of the brain's one thousand trillion neurological connections that control language, math, music, logic, and emotion.

As ancient wisdom goes, *we are what we think* (Proverbs 23:7, KJV). Experience shapes thought. Thought shapes mood. Mood shapes behavior. Behavior shapes relationships. Relationships—with God and man—shape destiny.

At some level, Bonnie understood the risks of her depleted inner world. She felt her own heart was too broken to be a safe scene for romantic love. She also carried a deep sense that she was unlovable, as her parents had convinced her of this through the habit of neglect and abuse.

Bonnie was twenty-eight when she met Trevor. They started out as friends, working together on church projects and missions trips. He was quiet, kind, and thoughtful.

Like her father, Trevor was a church deacon. But Bonnie quickly realized that men were like bottles: What mattered was not the label outside but the contents inside.

Trevor later said that Bonnie immediately won his heart. But he sensed she needed time—lots of time—to trust him. So he invited her to group events and to communal dinners in his home. She saw him stock his cabinets with snacks his friends liked, despite his different tastes. She observed his frequent favors for elderly or sick neighbors. Kindness was a way of life for Trevor. Kindness *was* Trevor. How could Bonnie resist?

Trevor offered Bonnie a love that blended four important elements, the same elements explored by C. S. Lewis in *The Four Loves*: friendship, affection, selfless care for her well-being, and, ultimately, romantic passion.[4] They married when she was thirty. Bonnie found a safe refuge in Trevor's heart and slowly began to heal and thrive emotionally. He, in turn, celebrated Bonnie's character, courage, spirit, and faith.

Without realizing it, Bonnie had discovered a major secret of emotional recovery: A good marriage can provide powerful compensation for a love-depleted childhood. When studying the various habits of loveless subjects who gradually overcame their past, Harvard researchers found that the loveless who thrived as adults were inevitably bolstered by a good marriage. But how could Bonnie attract such an appealing husband if she herself were damaged goods, as she feared?

STEPS TO HEALING

Bonnie's healing process had begun long before she ever met Trevor. In C. S. Lewis terms, perhaps that was the reason she was able to offer him *gift love,* a generous and responsive affection growing out of her respect and deep care for him. If she had remained depleted she would only have been able to offer *need love*, which rises out of a desperate and desolate heart. Such a soul hunger is never satisfied, since it is self-absorbed and ultimately cold to the longings of a partner's heart.

Bonnie was able to produce a well of gift love because years before meeting Trevor she had embarked on a journey to emotional health. In this process, Bonnie rewired her emotions by replacing family habits of coldness and neglect with surrogate family habits of warm, loving relationships.

She was able to import warmth in three ways. First, when urged by a counselor, she listed the heart-warmers in her life who had eased her pain, given her joy, and believed in her. There were teachers, school buddies, a coach, bosses, and a young stranger in Chicago who took her home for a warm bath, a hot dinner, and encouragement. (I was honored to make the list!)

Bonnie wrote a note to each heart-warmer on her list. She expressed gratitude for the kindness that became permanent insulation for her heart. She wrote letters in order to recycle some warmth back to those who had blessed her. As she wrote, tears of joy often flowed down her cheeks. When we reflect on old loves, those memories often stir or evoke powerful emotions tied to the people we are remembering (known as evocative memory). In Bonnie's case, those heart-soothing emotions flowed out of a revived sense of being loved, cherished, valued, and worthy of attention and care.

Second, Bonnie recruited surrogate family members for more imported warmth. She gravitated to a small town where she found fulfilling work and a boss who took personal interest in her and helped her outside of the workplace. She attended a church where members exuded belief in a loving God and accepted her, flaws and all. Drawn into a thriving faith community, she gained hope that perhaps vibrant life *was* possible as part of Christian experience, as Jesus promised (John 10:10). She found that the rejecting, punitive, judgmental faith of her father was simply fraud peddled in the name of Christ. Oh, how she loved the soothing touch of joy-filled hearts so unlike the harsh relationships of her childhood!

When we are old, our lives become the sum of all whom we have loved. It is important not to waste anyone.

GEORGE VAILLANT, *AGING WELL*

Bonnie's third step flowed naturally from the second. She imported warmth through a positive faith. In her church, she saw people who engaged life around them, smiled at the future, and warmed her world with joy flavored by goodness and grace. She found the exuberance and optimism of her faith family contagious and learned to trust God as a loving Father she had never known as a child. And before long, her vigorous faith gradually began to purge the fear-soaked theology and self-loathing seeded in her heart by a violent father.

By transplanting her heart and mind into nurturing

environments, the Bonnie who met Trevor was quite transformed from the Bonnie who first fled a toxic home.

The Trevor connection enabled a powerful fourth way of importing warmth to Bonnie's malnourished heart. Trevor's reliable love proved a potent antidote to spirit-stifling childhood abuse. Furthermore, she basked in the deep heat of love reflected back to her from four children. She was their sun, warming their world with affirmation, attention, guidance, and a joy for living. Their young hearts delighted in this nurturing, confidence-building mother who helped them love themselves as she loved them. They mirrored back to her the joyful affection she offered.

To this day Bonnie remains surprised and awed at the wonder of being loved by her husband and children.

But she has made that easy. Studies show four habits of effective family warmth that lead to positive relations inside and outside the family. Bonnie has excelled at them all:

1. **Frequent Warmth:** Bonnie's children (and husband) hear positive feedback from her daily. She cannot remember a single time her own parents praised her schoolwork, performance, or personal qualities. She is not repeating that spirit-stifling mistake.
2. **Specific Warmth:** "That's a very scary dinosaur you drew, Cal!" is more the type of feedback that Bonnie offers than "Nice picture." This mother offers her children specific affirmation that has a deeper impact.
3. **Intense Warmth:** Bonnie refuses to pollute praise to her children with fake or inflated credit. But if "Great

job!" "Super," "Way to go," or "That's our star!" fits, the words come easily. She knows the heartache of credit minimized or denied.

4. **Constructive Guidance:** Praise wrapped in truth has maximum credibility and impact. Bonnie often tells her children, "Practice that flute another twenty minutes." "Find two ways to improve your paper. I know you can." She doesn't dilute the empowering effect of warmth with spoken or unspoken distortion.

Studies show that Bonnie's habits are powerful in transforming loveless lives into cherished lives. She has made conscious choices to import soul-warming habits to nurture her own heart, and in the process she has become a maternal well from which her children draw strength.

Both Bonnie and Abraham Lincoln illustrate truths of human nature, which I believe are wired by our Creator. Inner healing can start with these simple steps of transformation:

PLAN FOR TRANSFORMATION

- **List your heart-warmers**
- **Recruit surrogate family**
- **Cultivate a positive faith**
- **Seek reliable love**

TRANSFORMING HABIT
Explore and resolve wounds from family history.

THREE

MOURNING LOSSES

As I sat nestled into a comfy box seat halfway up to the towering arena dome in Washington's MCI Center, my gaze was riveted to a speaker far below. His vastly enlarged face peered from giant screens as he pronounced tips for personal, financial, and spiritual security in an uncertain world. On this spring day in 1999, I had been allowed the use of a corporate box in order to host men from a workshop I facilitate every week just three blocks away at Gospel Rescue Ministries.

Suddenly, a roar of male voices filled the air behind me. I whirled to see a red blur coming through the hallway door into the twenty-seat box. The redness was rapidly engulfed by the cheering workshop group, who abandoned the speaker far below.

No wonder. The men, all homeless, were now eyeball to eyeball with Elizabeth Dole, former president of the American Red Cross, former U.S. secretary of transportation, former secretary of labor, and budding presidential candidate.

Minutes before, she had completed her own speech, an inspirational presentation on the subject of success.

Wrapping these men in her warm words and luminous smile, Mrs. Dole sank her ink pen into the sea of rescue-mission identity cards extended for her autograph. The men seemed delighted by their high-profile visitor, whose image is recognized around the world.

I was astounded.

Just three hours earlier, I had called her office with an unlikely request: After her speech, could she stop by the corporate box for a quick visit with a group of homeless men? Such a visit would inspire this bright and determined group, men who are working hard in a demanding recovery program to reclaim productive lives.

The inquiry had seemed both presumptuous and abrupt, factors I confessed to Elizabeth Dole's chief of staff. I knew her schedule is planned far in advance with great care and scrutiny. Surely she would be restricted by rigid demands on her time. I assumed she would not appear.

But there she was. No media. No public credit. No personal benefit from this unseen act to empower total strangers.

I was so very grateful for the powerful message her appearance sent to these displaced men: *You matter. Your life has value. You are worth this investment of time and energy.* Her presence honored the significance of lives on vastly different trajectories from her own.

Mrs. Dole soon departed, but such imported warmth had delivered one more tool for seeding charred inner worlds with new life. It's clear that a single nurturing encounter such as her visit can generate empowering memories for decades, and each caring experience feeds into a positive sense of self. As the men's lives intersected even briefly with good hearts from all social strata, my hope was that early messages of family and social rejection would be deflated, diluted, and over-ridden.

The arena box buzzed with excited reactions to Elizabeth Dole's visit, and the group exuded a tangible sense of joy. They finally turned their attention back to the speakers—except for deeply pensive Micah. His striking intelligence, dignity, and social sophistication demolished common perceptions of homeless men.

"What is it, Micah?" I inquired during a break from speeches.

Mostly he was perplexed. He was listening to strategies for personal and family success. But in his past, he had left two women who, he believed, had loved him deeply. Discarded with those women were three children he fathered. "Family success" seemed far out of reach for Micah and for those he had ejected from his life.

"Why would I do this?" he now wondered. He was lonely in his isolation. He knew those lost loves and children also suffered from the emotional, financial, and social trauma of abandonment. His children floundered among shattered dreams of a warm niche in their father's heart. Their self-esteem was sabotaged by waves of indignities and suffering spawned by rejection, as their father chose distance and silence over a close connection to them.

Now, after months in the intensive mission rehabilitation program, Micah finally asked himself a tough question: *Why did I abandon partners who were rocks in my life—people who were loving, kind, and considerate? Why am I denying precious children their father?* He seemed repulsed by his own bad judgment and defective life skills that had somehow dumped him into a deep well of despair.

Although we were surrounded by thousands in this gargantuan arena, it was as if we had been transported to a very private niche in Micah's heart, a hidden place that seemed desperate for healing. Such heart repair was doable if he was ready for tough soul-searching, mind-stretching, habit-changing work.

Micah seemed committed to a journey toward wholeness. This excursion would compel him to examine old family habits, to scrutinize his own choices, and to summon courage for change. He was resolute. His face seemed to signal, *I'm ready. Let's roll.*

FACE FAMILY REALITIES

Carefully, I posed a question. "You seem especially troubled by lost relationships with your children, Micah. Is this true?" He nodded.

"Would you like to explore some ways to ease the grief from broken relationships with your kids?"

Micah nodded again. He was with me.

As odd as it may seem, in order to ease Micah's present pain, we needed to start with his past, using his history to light a path to the future. We needed to look back further than the broken connections with his own children.

"Tell me about your experience with your own father."

Micah's eyes seemed to flicker with a new sense of sorrow.

"He left me, my two brothers, my new baby sister, and my mother when I was four," said Micah.

"So how did you observe a healthy relationship between a man and woman or between a father and son?"

"I didn't."

"How did your family survive when your father left?"

"My mother worked two jobs to pay the rent and bills."

"So when you lost your father, you lost your mother, too?"

"Yes. To work."

"If your mother worked two jobs, who raised you?"

Micah's eyes widened. His voice softened. His mind was carrying him back to a very vulnerable time in a little boy's life. "I raised myself."

"Let me understand this. Your father was gone. Your mother was mostly gone. You raised yourself. Who raised your two younger brothers and little sister?"

"I had to take care of them, too."

"So the child-you raised you, plus your brothers and sister. As a very little boy, you became the parent of four children. Do you see how this can help explain some of your trouble now?"

"We just existed. No one really taught me how to live."

"Exactly. So think carefully here. You've made some choices that have been very painful for you and for others. But if a child raised you, maybe it's amazing you do as well as you do. You've held good jobs and made good money. You're a superior communicator. You connect well with people around you. In many ways, you seem remarkable."

A faint smile softened Micah's expression. But sorrow and remorse still clouded his state of mind.

I wanted to look back a bit further to see what else we might discover. "What do you know of your *father's* history?" I asked.

A pensive look filtered across Micah's face. "My mother told me that when he was seven, my father and his two brothers woke up in this little Southern town and both their parents were gone. Just disappeared. People in a church took them in, but in many ways they were on their own."

"So how did your father learn about a thriving marriage or warm parent-child relationships?"

"How did he? How could he?"

"Indeed. How could he? What about two or three generations before your father—what about those parent-child relations?"

"They were slaves . . ."

"Right. So you may not know with certainty, but based on historic accounts what do you think was likely?"

"Families were torn apart, husbands from wives, parents from children."

"You asked how you could possibly leave loving women and sons who needed you. Are you getting any answers to those questions?"

"Sure. I've never seen good relationships and ran off when I became uncomfortable."

In ten minutes Micah had catalogued generations of wounds that had caused massive emotional and social hemorrhaging in his family. His losses were profound:

- The loss of childhood, annihilated by adult duties
- The loss of a father's touch on Micah's mind and heart

- The loss of any model of adult male productivity or responsibility
- The loss of an emotionally available mother
- The loss of trust, as relationships inevitably led to exploitation and abuse
- The loss of any refuge when he was hurt, struggling, confused, or scared, with nowhere to go but back into himself
- The loss of home, as Micah was psychologically homeless from his earliest memory
- The loss of self-esteem shaped by available, nurturing, instructive adults
- The loss of safety, with no protection from violent abuse by bigger neighbor boys
- The loss of competence in lasting, mature relationships, which he had never seen or experienced
- The loss of a healthy self, as both his father and mother misdefined him in their minds and in his as a tiny parent surrogate unworthy of care and support
- The loss of capacity for emotional intimacy, which requires a healthy sense of self and ability not only to initiate relationships, but to sustain them beyond conflict and pain

CONFESS THE SINS OF THE FATHERS

As Micah and I talked, our exchange was shaped by pronounced sorrow. Each question prompted painful images. Each response led to another probing question. This family history was riddled with suffering and grief. Following the laws of life, wounds in distant generations—some self-inflicted and some inflicted by others—reverberated through generations down the line.

They . . . confessed their sins and the wickedness of their fathers.
NEHEMIAH 9:2

Why dig up the past? Why not just forgive and forget?

"Big mistake! Hold it! Don't go there!" the ancient Jewish leader Nehemiah might have shouted back if he had been featured at the success conference we attended. In Nehemiah 9, he demonstrated how to take a "moral inventory," not just of personal life, but of family history, a challenge issued millennia before Alcoholics Anonymous and others discovered the power of this healing strategy.

"Confess the sins of the fathers" is the way Nehemiah framed this transforming habit. But how does that work? How exactly does one confess others' sins or wounds?

Detective skills help. Gently prying ancient history out of older relatives and extended family will take some diplomatic and investigative skill, but the following questions are a good place to start:

- What did parents, grandparents, aunts, uncles, and siblings do that damaged their own position in the family or wounded others?
- Who were the underresponsible or coddled ones in the family?
- Which ones were overresponsible or rescuers?

- What health, financial, or legal crises rocked the family?
- How did outsiders traumatize or abuse the family?
- How were children nurtured, or how were they treated as property to use, abuse, or discard?
- How did such actions damage financial security, destroy marriages, wound children, shut off employment or social acceptance, and create waves of fear, rage, failure, or despair in the family?
- Who were the family favorites or heroes? How were they treated?
- Who were the family scapegoats and how were they treated?

NEHEMIAH DEMON-STRATED HOW TO TAKE A "MORAL INVENTORY," NOT JUST OF PERSONAL LIFE, BUT OF FAMILY HISTORY, A CHALLENGE ISSUED MILLENNIA BEFORE ALCOHOLICS ANONYMOUS AND OTHERS DISCOVERED THE POWER OF THIS HEAL-ING STRATEGY.

- How did the family view religious faith? As a means of access to a personal God who could and would intervene in their life? Or as an inherited obligation or irrelevant mystery or fraud?

It's okay to name names. Assign responsibility. Face the facts. Nehemiah gave us permission as he detailed how ancient Israelites should pursue this soul-cleansing, mind-clarifying process. A complete summary of Nehemiah's thoughts on recovering a family's legacy is explained in the sidebar on page 92.

What if you refuse? What if you'd rather leave the past in the past?

Such denial of personal history, notes Dan Allendar in *The Wounded Heart*, is somewhat like a self-inflicted frontal lobot-omy.[1] Truth-squelching deadens our mental ability to scrutinize, measure, and evaluate experiences that have wired our own personal perceptions, expectations, emotions, reactions, choices, and relationships. It is a dumbing down of self, producing a sort of "social dementia"—the inability to think, judge, or choose coherently because our thoughts are flowing out of distorted assumptions.

> DENIAL OF PERSONAL HISTORY IS SOMEWHAT LIKE A SELF-INFLICTED FRONTAL LOBOTOMY.

As for Micah, he was ready to stop the cycle. Like Rip van Winkle awakening from a stupor, he had scrutinized not only his past, but also its impact on his personality and relationships.

What about history's impact on Micah's destiny from that point on? That greatly depended on Micah. The choice for healing was now up to him.

EXAMINE ONGOING FALLOUT

Over the next few weeks, Micah began to explore the habits of his life that served only to deepen old wounds or dig new ones. He described repeated dead-end relationships with loves, friends, and employers. He realized that usually it was he who rejected, who left, who abandoned. But he also found that the break was often preceded by a request from others to give back a bit of care or attention.

It was as if Micah had calculated an unpaid debt and revolted when others, at last, refused to pay. The debt was racked up by parents who left him emotionally impoverished. Somewhere in Micah's heart he knew he had been cheated. The debt had been psychologically recorded, totaled, and compounded with interest over the years. Although Micah *consciously* assigned the debt to his parents, he *subconsciously* shoved the bill at anyone else who wandered into his life.

Most significantly, Micah had billed the women in his life. These motherly lovers were drawn to a man who made them feel valued and necessary by his covert neediness. He was smart, physically imposing, and, in many ways, competent. But while appearing a bastion of male strength, Micah siphoned life energy from doting women in subtle ways. The women were comforted, at first, by a false sense of security. But in time, they grew physically and spiritually weary of one-way emotional support and began to seek more reciprocal caring, more mutuality in the relationship.

When Micah was asked to *give* emotional support, he bolted. A familiar but terrifying sensation shoved him away. He was unnerved by deep inner forebodings of impending doom. When very young, he was coerced to play adult roles and meet adult needs—which was mission impossible for a small child. Such demands were a form of rejection, a refusal to offer a small child the care he required, while blaming and punishing him when he failed in adult duties. Now fully grown, he was expected to perform as a husband, father, and worker—which should have been normal at his age. But he was so destitute emotionally that minor requests from others seemed treacherous, even malevolent. He used distance to increase safety and decrease his pain, leaving baffled lovers, children, bosses, and colleagues behind.

What if this pattern continued? What if Micah continued to flee at the first sign of accountability in a relationship?

"I'll be very lonely," acknowledged Micah. "I'll never *keep* relationships."

TAKE CHARGE AND CHANGE

Micah could not rewrite history or coerce his aging mother or father to give him long overdue care. But he *could* control his choices.

Examining his own pain, Micah could now better comprehend the wounds he had left in his children's fragile hearts. He could not deny that his decisions had emotionally violated his own children, even if his failures did grow out of ancient family history.

If they will confess their sins and the sins of their fathers . . .
for their sake I will remember the covenant with their ancestors.
LEVITICUS 26:40, 45

Micah felt driven to compensate as much as possible for his mistakes. He was compelled to connect with the grown children he long ago deserted, but he also seemed paralyzed by anxiety. "Why would they want to see me?" he asked, noting his status in a homeless program.

The other mission residents urged Micah to reach out to his long-lost sons, and within days he announced that his eighteen-year-old son was coming to meet him for lunch. "He couldn't wait to see me, but I'm nervous about this lunch," said Micah.

The lunch went well—so well, in fact, that they began to meet regularly at the insistence of Micah's son. Soon Micah connected with his other two sons and their mothers, who were both remarried. Micah was astonished that all of them welcomed his reemergence into their life, and that even their husbands were open to him.

How did Micah explain reactions full of such grace, so lacking in anger or bitterness?

"They're all active in church," said Micah, with reddened eyes. "What a gift to me, that their faith guides them in this response."

Now came the tough part: Micah learned that the father who abandoned him, now ninety years old, lived a hundred miles away in Richmond, Virginia. Micah longed to see his father but struggled with deep resentment from his own abandonment.

One of his sons offered to drive Micah to Richmond, staging a reunion of three generations.

"When I knocked on that apartment door I felt mostly anguish and fear," reported Micah later. "But as the door opened, my father's face was so full of anxiety that my heart melted. I could see that he was scared, too. He was seeing a son he had abandoned who might hate him. He had wanted to see me before he died, and here I was. We had a wonderful visit and talk on the phone a lot now. I feel liberated, as if a burden is lifted off my shoulders. Finally, I have a father. I feel more grounded, more at peace."

A month later, Micah admitted that he had new anxiety over closer family relationships. His eighteen-year-old son was meeting him two or three times weekly. After years of painful separation, Micah found that he still struggled with fear. "I'm scared," he said of the father-son companionship.

What could be so scary about being *wanted?* How many forty-nine-year-old dads long to be invited into their son's heart and life?

"Are you afraid of annihilation, Micah?"

Micah was bound in silence, his eyes locked to mine as he probed within for an answer.

"Yes," he responded quietly. "That's exactly it."

"Are you afraid that for once you'll let this boy deep into your heart—but someday he'll reject you and you won't survive?"

"Yes," said Micah.

"Would it feel safer just to lock him out now, before he moves in deeper?"

"Yes."

"How often have you done that in other relationships?"

"A lot."

"What's the result?"

"Loneliness. Despair."

"So this is a big choice. For more of the same loneliness and despair, keep doing the same: Lock people out. If you ever want lasting relationships, you have to risk your heart. There's no other way."

So went our discussions several years ago. At the time, Micah's choices were very difficult. But he realized that in order to transform his habit of rejection—a habit he was able to trace back to his forefathers and to the society in which they lived—he needed to take some risks. He chose new habits of life and is now living with the consequences.

Today, Micah has grown closer to his sons. He is deeply comforted by regular contact with his father. He has held a rewarding job for two years. At times he is wounded, and

> IN ORDER TO TRANS-
> FORM HIS HABIT OF
> REJECTION — A HABIT
> HE WAS ABLE TO TRACE
> BACK TO HIS FORE-
> FATHERS AND TO THE
> SOCIETY IN WHICH THEY
> LIVED — HE NEEDED TO
> TAKE SOME RISKS.

at times, he wounds. But he refuses to flee. He faces the pain, talks out the conflict, and works at resolution.

Micah isn't the sort of guy featured on the success conference marquee. For that, they recruit the rich, the famous, or the professional superstars. But the conference (and the rest of us) could learn a thing or two from Micah, who has grown far beyond the man I met in 1999.

Micah has demonstrated major keys to personal and family success:

1. **Dig out the facts of family history**—the good, the bad, and the ugly. Truth does set us free, sending ripples of empowerment throughout the family system.
2. **Mourn losses, grieve old pain, lance festering psychological wounds, and drain out emotional and relational**

toxins. Allow yourself to mourn—for self, for others wounded by family history, and for the victims of your own destructive choices.

3. **Examine ongoing fallout from the destructive habits repeated generation after generation.** Calculate escalating costs of treacherous family habits.

4. **Take responsibility for choices, the habits of life that layer after layer become character.** Pay now or pay later. Pay now by tough changes to your one controllable person: you. Pay now by accountability for damage inflicted on others, or pay later through corroded emotions and crippled relationships left as a result of an undisciplined life.

As a family counselor and workshop facilitator, I have coached hundreds of people through this process—from the homeless to corporate executives; males and females; inner-city and suburban dwellers; teenagers, parents, and great-grandparents; Protestants, Catholics, Copts, Jews, Muslims, and agnostics.

I am awed by those who choose to become the redemptive generation. As M. Scott Peck's phenomenal best seller says, they choose the road less traveled, a path that requires courage, integrity, and grit. "No more!" they say to pain in themselves and in their families. "It will stop *now*. With *me*. I will no longer torture myself or cripple others."

Such stellar souls choose Micah's way—a priceless gift to themselves and a treasured legacy to their children and grandchildren.

And the emotional, spiritual, and relational power trickles on down. Stem by stem. Branch by branch. Right down the family tree.

PLAN FOR TRANSFORMATION

- **Face family realities**
- **Confess past family sins**
- **Examine consequences of multigenerational family habits**
- **Take charge and change**

TRANSFORMING HABIT

Find reason to celebrate, even in your grief.

FOUR

CELEBRATE AND EMBRACE GOOD GRIEF

It has been said that he who controls your past controls your future. That's a point worthy of contemplation, but also this: Mere *perceptions* (accurate or not) of people and events of the past can rule our beliefs, relationships, and responses, all of which shape destiny.

In Sharon's case, early memories of her parents and childhood relationships were like gloomy clouds that hung over every aspect of her existence. She struggled with obsessive-compulsive tendencies and depression, finally seeking counseling in hopes of breaking free from the pain in her life. Her striking intelligence, impressive professional credentials, and keen spiritual insights seemed stalled by an immobilizing sorrow.

During every counseling session, one subject always came up: Sharon's deep grief over the favor her parents showered on her older sister, Christine, and the crumbs of affection they only occasionally dribbled Sharon's way. Since childhood, Christine had been treated as the family princess, given a lovely bedroom, beautiful clothes, and generous attention from both her mother and father. In comparison, Sharon seemed relegated to second-class status. Her bedroom was cluttered with cardboard boxes storing family property, her clothes were nothing special, and her parents offered only tiny morsels of care.

At thirty-nine, Sharon still strived to earn her parents' favor. Although she lived two thousand miles from her elderly parents, she still called them every day and granted them great influence over her. If her parents said, "Don't take trains," she avoided trains. If they needed help, she rushed to the rescue. When they were ill, she took time off work to care for them: cooking, cleaning, and waiting on them. But even then, they showed little appreciation, simply waving at her as she went out the door to the airport while their ears, focus, and affection were glued by phone connection to Christine. No matter how much Sharon slaved away, she was instantly discarded when Christine wanted attention.

One day during a counseling session, Sharon and I charted her family on a board, outlining each sister's track record with marriage, jobs, children, and other relationships.

Both sisters were married.

Both sisters had children.

Both sisters had earned advanced degrees and demonstrated superior intelligence.

But one sister had been married three times, striking out twice. The same sister had alienated numerous relatives, other than the parents. Her life was laced with turbulent, conflicted, unreliable relationships, which profoundly affected the overall flavor and direction of her life.

Who would that be? The princess or the pauper, as defined by riches of parental "love" bestowed?

As it happened, Princess Christine had been through two divorces and all the emotional, psychological, and financial trauma that goes with shattered marriages and families. Extended family members deeply distrusted and resented her, weary of her wounding behaviors.

MASTER YOUR MEMORIES

"Is there any connection between Christine's history with your parents and her sad marriages and family relationships?" I asked Sharon.

"I think she expects everyone else to cater to her the way my parents did. Her husbands and others refuse, and she becomes alienated," said Sharon.

"Look at this board," I said, pointing to broken relationships now shown graphically around Christine's symbol on the family chart. "Every session, you seem filled with grief that you do not have the life of your sister."

"I know," said Sharon quietly.

"You seem so sad that you did not have the same kind of parental love."

"I know."

"Are you still convinced you are the loser in this picture?"

"I think maybe the love she had wasn't so good after all. Maybe it was destructive."

"Maybe so! What if you had been treated the same, given the same kind of love as Christine?"

"I might have turned out the same, with broken marriages and negative relationships."

RELATIONSHIPS, SAYS C. S. LEWIS IN *The Four Loves*, OFFER A SCHOOL OF VIRTUE OR A SCHOOL OF VICE.

"Do you still regret so much your role in this family?"

"Maybe I'm very fortunate. Maybe I was protected. Maybe even as a child, God was looking out for me." Sharon seemed relieved, awed, and deeply grateful at the possibility that her "unfortunate" neglect had saved her from the plight of her pampered sister.

Within one hour, the face of Sharon's world had changed.

She stopped calling her parents every day, an action that had been rooted in her own desperate desire for slivers of their attention. Within days, they began calling her, a confirmation that they might value her more and even seek connection if she quit pursuing so hard.

Sharon began riding trains and embracing other actions disapproved by her parents but normal for a thirty-nine-year-old matriarch of her own family. Her parents adjusted to this "new" daughter and reduced their demands that she capitulate to their every whim.

Sharon's self-confidence improved, and within weeks she secured a job, where her impressive intellect and gifts not only generated additional affirmation of her worth but also enhanced her family's income. As for obsessive-compulsive hoarding, she soon shipped out mounds of outdated clothes and excess stuff from her house.

Distorted images of the past had controlled Sharon's life and threatened her future. She had idealized her parents and overrated the affection they showered on her sister. She had devalued herself as a child deemed unworthy of these elevated parental figures. She had steeped her mind in sorrow for a lost love that was neither so loving nor such a loss after all. She had accepted a victim identity when it was her sister who had been much more crippled by toxic relationships in the home.

Twisted childhood relationships controlled her past, and as a result, they also controlled her future. As she scrutinized her family's bonds through a prism of truth, Sharon realized that distasteful soul medicine had actually inoculated her against toxic family habits.

Relationships, says C. S. Lewis in *The Four Loves*, offer a school of virtue or a school of vice. In Sharon's case, her parents ran a school of vice for both daughters, favored and neglected. They pampered Christine in ways that gave her an inflated view of herself and an entitlement mentality, sabotaging key relationships in her life. They devalued Sharon in ways that gave her a bleak view of herself, of the world around her, and of her expectations of the future.

BE GRATEFUL FOR GOOD GRIEF

The lessons Sharon learned in her parents' homeschool of neglect could only be erased when she gained a clearer perspective. She embraced the wisdom of Nazi concentration-camp survivor and renowned psychiatrist Viktor Frankl, which he spelled out in his book *The Doctor and the Soul*: Suffering can radically enhance emotional awareness of what *ought not to be* while clarifying what *ought to be* found in genuine love, righteousness, and justice. Sharon learned to use her sad family saga for insights about how not to live as well as how to live and how to love.

Especially powerful was Sharon's new ability to celebrate "good grief." Her grief arose from years of parental neglect. But she concluded that in some ways this was good grief because her parents seemed to care for their children in one of two extremes: *neglect* or *coddling indulgence.* After seeing the destructive impact of coddling indulgence on her sister's life, Sharon became grateful that her childhood experience had been less damaging than it might have been.

Shedding her family's oppressive ways, Sharon seemed like a caterpillar shucking its cocoon to emerge transformed. As a companion on her journey, I watched a remarkable personal revolution, as a stifled but gifted personality was set free by thoughtful reconstruction of dark memories.

One of the most potent . . . antidotes to depression is seeing things differently, or cognitive reframing. . . . In other words, seeing the loss differently, in a more positive light—is an antidote to the sadness.

DANIEL GOLEMAN, *EMOTIONAL INTELLIGENCE*

Sharon is like an updated version of the Old Testament's Joseph after he suffered family trauma (Genesis 37, 39–45). Confronting his brothers, who were terrified of retaliation for selling him as a slave, Joseph soothed their fears with his revised take on family treachery. "You intended to harm me," he said, "but God intended it for good" (Genesis 50:20).

It was the brothers' evil that launched Joseph as an unlikely political power in Egypt, positioned to save not only himself, but also his estranged family, from destruction. As he rose from prison inmate to the top of the political strata, Joseph concluded: "God has made me forget . . . all my father's household" (Genesis 41:51).

An important point here is blurred in language translation. Later events proved that Joseph didn't forget his conniving family at all! But any bitterness over his family's betrayal waned as his memories were mellowed by a growing awareness of the big picture. God had used his brothers' treachery not only to save his neck, but also to catapult him into a stunning career.

CONQUER DARK THOUGHTS

Joseph's memories of his brothers' abuse caused him pain until newer, positive life experiences diluted the hurt. Sharon endured decades of emotional suffering generated in her own mind, which was riveted to painful interpretations of family history. Relief came as she conquered these dark thought habits. As Herbert Benson of the Harvard Medical School notes, such mastery of the mind is a secret to soothing emotional pain, squelching terror, and even preventing death.

Exploring the subject both scientifically and personally, Benson recounts in vivid detail a terrifying experience from his days as a young doctor. He was examining an Asian patient for the first time when he broke into a sweat, became nauseated, and felt his heart rate surge.

Why would a young doctor be flooded by full-blown panic-attack symptoms at the sight of a total stranger?

"I don't believe I know you, but I had this very intense and strange reaction upon seeing you," Benson informed his patient. There was a possible explanation, replied the man, as detailed in Benson's book, *Timeless Healing: The Power and Biology of Belief.* During World War II, the patient had been featured in Hollywood movies as Tokyo Joe, a fighter pilot who shot down American planes and pilots. The actor was also cast as a villain in scores of other movies Benson had seen as a child.[1]

While the doctor did not consciously recognize his new patient, his unconscious mind was jolted by a mix of ominous foreboding and emotion tied to movies he had seen as a child. Deeply buried memories held enormous power over Herbert Benson's sense of identity as a powerless victim, over his perceptions of the world around him (a scary place), and over his anticipation of the future (at imminent risk from a fearsome personality).

As Dr. Benson discovered, troubling memories can generate waves of anxiety and fear long after the original trauma. But his emotions shifted radically as he reorganized autobiographical memory, the version of his life story within his own mind. As he tells us, his self-story was not fully accurate. He had *not* encountered a truly dangerous villain in the movies, so he was *not* in danger when the same guy appeared in his office. Reactions of fear in his mind and body stopped when his mind embraced revised history.

Research has found that such mental reorganizing can dramatically reconstruct personality, the part of us that is so powerfully molded by individual *perceptions* of life experience.[2] We've already seen this process in Sharon. As she edited the self-history in her mind, hope, energy, and joy displaced despair, inertia, and depression. Her internal transformation soon enhanced personal and professional relationships.

CHERISH THE GIFT OF A LESSER EVIL

The ability to find meaning and hope in suffering offers a powerful secret to mental health and survival, notes Viktor Frankl, a survivor of Auschwitz, Dachau, and less-notorious Nazi death camps.[3] Holocaust victims who survived the war the most intact mentally, observes Frankl, were those who recognized that some forms of their trauma were an escape from even more horrific terror. These survivors were able to draw inspiration and strength from affliction.

Such was the case when one group of Nazi prisoners was transferred from the loathsome Auschwitz death factory to another notorious camp, as Frankl describes in *Man's Search for Meaning*. Frankl reports that 90 percent of the prisoners who arrived with him at Auschwitz died within hours; first gassed in fake showers, then reduced to ashes in giant crematoria. After months of torture and brutal forced labor, survivors were herded into trains. They were terrified that they were being transferred to an even more ghastly Nazi camp. Unbelievable as it may seem, Frankl reports that the prisoners jammed into train cars broke into a "dance of joy" upon realizing they were headed *only* for Dachau.

Dachau was known as a site of unspeakable horror, but Frankl and his fellow prisoners celebrated their arrival because it was rated a lesser evil than the alternative Mauthausen camp across the Danube River. The prisoners welcomed Dachau because at the time it had no killing ovens, no crematorium, and no gas. "This joyful surprise put us all in a good mood," says Frankl. "We had come . . . to a camp which did not have a 'chimney.'"

NOT ONLY CAN SUFFERING "LOSE ITS STING" WHEN ITS MEANING IS CLARIFIED, IT CAN ACTUALLY BECOME CAUSE FOR CELEBRATION WHEN MINED FOR GOLD BURIED UNDER THE RUBBLE OF PAIN AND SORROW.

While at the fearsome Dachau, Frankl says, "We were grateful for the smallest of mercies," such as being stripped naked in a hut so frigid that icicles hung from the ceiling. But the hut's "mercy" was a delousing treatment, a purging of bothersome parasites.

As Frankl notes, suffering loses its sting "once we form a clear and precise picture of it." Not only can suffering be lessened when its meaning is clarified, it can actually become cause for celebration when it is mined for gold buried under the rubble of pain and sorrow.

Perhaps none of us will ever endure atrocities even close to those of Frankl's death camps. But those who wring hope out of such despair, pry light out of darkness, and seize trauma as an escape from even worse suffering offer all of us priceless lessons for triumph over human anguish.

DEFUSE A TERMINAL STATE OF MIND

Intrigued by his own experiences showing the mind's great power over the body, Herbert Benson was compelled to study it further. He found that thought habits are extremely powerful, so powerful, in fact, that some can prove deadly. Benson cites Dr. George Engel, formerly on the University of Rochester medical faculty, who reported more than one hundred cases of sudden death produced by an apparent sense of powerlessness and inability to cope with life.[4]

In addition to torture, starvation, work, weather, and epidemics, the loss of hope is believed to have been a major cause of death among Nazi concentration-camp prisoners; that is, many suffered from a terminal state of mind.

For those prisoners not slaughtered outright, the war against their tormentors was won or lost on the battlefront of the mind. Survivors who not only lived but thrived once free were described as those able to:

- Escape into an inner world of faith
- Seek identity in spiritual values, not circumstances
- Celebrate minor victories
- Thrive in the comfort of worthy companions sharing a torturous journey
- Express gratitude for whatever was not taken from them
- Cling to hope for the future
- Savor the tiniest bits of beauty, even if accessed only by memory
- Diminish the impact of horror by focusing elsewhere

- Tap humor for relief, despite macabre circumstances
- Use suffering as a source of growth
- Relish what no Nazi could destroy—the love of family and friends
- Find meaning in pain and suffering[5]

From any other source, challenging battered, bruised, and sorrow-soaked victims to emulate these mind strategies might seem naive, patronizing, or even cruel. But those who are weary, teary, bitter, and deflated due to wounds inflicted in the family or elsewhere would be wise to tune in to Nazi-defying survivors. They thrived mentally, professionally, and personally after years of unspeakable suffering, because they were determined to siphon light from darkness and wring hope from despair.

Be made new in the attitude of your minds. . . . Get rid of all bitterness, rage and anger, brawling and slander, along with every form of malice. EPHESIANS 4:23, 31

As M. Scott Peck tells us, taking this road less traveled requires personal accountability for one's condition, regardless of circumstances. Those who shift their focus from life's villains and misfortune to their own responsibility "find themselves not only cured and free from the curses of their childhood and ancestry but also find themselves living in a new and different world," declares Peck. "What they once perceived as problems they now perceive as opportunities."[6]

This is not academic theory or psychobabble. It is truth

wrapped in the skin of many counseling clients, including Sharon, and of such trauma survivors as Viktor Frankl. It is truth etched in Scripture through the life of Joseph. And it is truth that paves a path to inner peace for those who dare to take this higher way.

PLAN FOR TRANSFORMATION

- Identify treasures you have gained through pain:

Character	Vision
Perseverance	Wisdom
Faith	Compassion
Drive	

- List ways that specific times of suffering or disappointment may have saved you from worse sorrow
- Use faith to triumph over trauma and evil:
  Prayer
  Personal and communal Bible study
  Seeking God's direction
- Express gratitude in a journal and/or to God for specific gifts to the spirit, mind, and character gained through trials and sorrow

TRANSFORMING HABIT
Define your own role in your extended
and nuclear family.

FIVE

ACTIVATE A FAMILY FREEDOM FORMULA

"I wonder if there aren't two groups of us," mused one partici-
pant at a 1967 family research conference. "Those who . . .
leave home and never come back, and those who stay home
and never go away."[1]

These are two extreme but common responses to family influence. One extreme uses feet to do the talking, moving far
away from the parental household or otherwise choosing
physical or emotional distance as protection from family demands or control.

At the other extreme are those who can't (or won't) take a
stand on personal convictions in the family. They stay home
emotionally no matter where they are physically. They abandon personal judgment regarding their role in the parental
family and sometimes even their role in their own marriages
and in society. Within the family they remain childlike, never
really developing independent convictions or adult behavior.

People at both extremes sacrifice thriving family relationships and roles. They also squelch healthy scrutiny and revision of toxic or counterproductive family habits.

So how does one find that middle ground? The Family Freedom Formula is a tool that anyone can use to find a healthy role within his or her family. As you will see through the case of six-foot-three bodybuilder Jesse, the formula only requires a few doses of clarity, integrity, courage, and resolve.

THE FAMILY FREEDOM FORMULA IS A TOOL THAT ANYONE CAN USE TO FIND A HEALTHY ROLE WITHIN HIS OR HER FAMILY. IT ONLY REQUIRES A FEW DOSES OF CLARITY, INTEGRITY, COURAGE, AND RESOLVE.

When Jesse arrived in my office a few years ago, he carried two secrets no casual observer would likely guess: First, thirty-three-year-old Jesse was a recovering cocaine addict. Second, he was fresh from jail on drug charges and had been diverted into my orbit by a Virginia judge.

Sizing up Jesse's prospects for an addiction-recovery program, I noted some valuable assets: his willingness to assume responsibility for risky habits, his history of reliable employment, his strong network of drug-free friends, and a family that appeared to be caring and supportive.

As it turned out, Jesse's battle to rebuild a stable life was sabotaged by a surprising culprit: his adoring but overly dependent mother.

At sixty-three, Mom headed a household still sheltering Jesse's two brothers, a thirty-year-old carpenter and a thirty-five-year-old auto mechanic. But when house or auto crises hit, this matriarch inevitably bypassed her two handy sons to seek a rescue from Jesse. Renting a room five miles away from his family, Jesse was a mechanical klutz who unfortunately left pipes, engines, and appliances worse off than he found them.

So why did his mother depend on Jesse, Mr. Fix-It Fiasco? Habits in this family had little to do with skill, reliability, or even finances. Choices were not driven by logic, but by a desperate pursuit of emotional security. Abandoned by her husband, this mom clung to Jesse as a surrogate spouse. She soaked up Jesse's kindness, hoping to anesthetize a soul grieved by loneliness and rejection.

Mom's unrestrained demands on Jesse were no act of love, but neither was his injudicious sacrifice of himself to satisfy these demands. Assuming responsibility for an adult relative who exaggerated her helplessness, Jesse put his job, his economic security, and his recovery in jeopardy.

His boss grew increasingly agitated as Jesse took more and more time off for family-rescue missions. With stress mounting, Jesse felt tempted to lurch for the addict's escape into drugs. That choice would likely land Jesse back behind bars, a prospect that would devastate not only him but also his mother.

If it was so treacherous, why did Jesse allow others to stick him with the family rescuer job? Why do any of us allow others to impose roles destructive to ourselves and even to them?

THE PERILS OF PSEUDOINTIMACY

As is true in many relationships, Jesse and his mother had established a false intimacy based on distorted images of one another. The mother acted as if she was helpless and inadequate, which she was not. The son accepted the role of family hero, as if he had the resources for perpetual rescue missions, which he did not.

Mother and son lurched their way through a cherished but toxic relationship. They avoided true emotional intimacy, which at its core required being honest with themselves and with each other. This pair functioned as a parasite and host: The mother siphoned power from her son's limited emotional resources, sapping him of energy essential for his own survival.

Let the winds of the heavens dance between you.
Love one another, but make not a bond of love:
Let it rather be a moving sea between the
shores of your souls. . . .
And stand together, yet not too near together:
For the pillars of the temple stand apart,
And the oak tree and the cypress grow not in
each other's shadow.

KAHLIL GIBRAN, *THE PROPHET*

Contrasted with selfless gift love, such narcissistic need love, observes C. S. Lewis, leads to self-indulgent expectations beyond reason. Those who choose helplessness as a life habit can wield enormous power over the destinies of those who passively yield to such control. Jesse's mother helped set a drug and penal trap for her precious son, and he reinforced her chronic neediness.

Contrary to the loving image they presented to outsiders,

Jesse and his mother were coconspirators in a dance of mutual destruction. Desperate for survival, Jesse agreed to try the seven-point Family Freedom Formula. The formula focuses on personal conviction and behaviors, not on changing others. Remarkably, when you don't try to force your needs on others but make constructive shifts to your own role, you are likely to see healthy changes infuse your family, even if it is deeply resistant to change. To work, however, the process must have integrity. When the hidden motive of self-change is to coerce others, the human heart has a way of detecting and revolting against such manipulation.

FAMILY FREEDOM FORMULA

Adaptable to Various Life Situations

1. Decide who you really are or should be in your family and what that means in terms of your behavior. (Contrast your *assigned* family role to the role you *choose*.)

2. Inform affected parties in positive terms of the behavior you are choosing.

3. Expect anger shown through silence, withdrawal, verbal attacks, or other hostile responses, because your behavior change may *feel* like rejection to others.

4. Avoid the temptation to blame, counterattack, defend yourself, or make excuses.

5. Initiate affirming contact with the angry party or parties, and through action disprove rejection.

6. Give the shift time: weeks, months, years.

7. Expect readjustment, maturation, and stabilization of the entire family system. Allow time for relationship transformation.

Below are the formula's steps to liberation, followed by Jesse's application of the principles.

JESSE'S PERSONALIZED PLAN

Jesse's version of the liberation formula looked like this:

1. **Adopt a chosen role, not an imposed role.** "I want to be a responsible adult in this family," said Jesse, "not the rescuer." For Jesse, choosing responsibility meant shedding the overresponsibility imposed by family expectations.

2. **Inform your family members of your choice.** In a meeting with his mother, Jesse offered specific guidelines for his support in the future. "I'm good at accounting, at painting, and at being a companion when you're in the mood for dinner or a movie. So on Saturday or Sunday or other days after 6 PM I can fit into the picture this way. But I'm lousy at plumbing, electrical stuff, car engines, and appliance repair. So I'm not going to tackle those jobs anymore," said Jesse, suggesting his brothers or paid repairmen as options.

3. **Expect anger.** Dropping her habit of phoning Jesse daily, his mother stopped calling at all and offered chilly silence when he called her. "I thought I could depend on you, but now I know better," she said, sniffing.

4. **Avoid blame or defensiveness.** Jesse could have blamed his drug peril on his mother's evasion of normal adult

functions. He could have whined that he'd been far more responsive to her than his brothers had. But such reactions would have shifted the focus away from Jesse's healthy choice for adult responsibility. Accusations or defensiveness would have reinforced his mother's perceptions that he was insensitive.

"I know it's hard for you to figure out new solutions, but this is a better balance for both of us," said Jesse, sticking to his decision but refusing to indulge in blame or excuses.

5. **Initiate affirming contact with the angry party.** What could reassure Jesse's mother of his continuing love and commitment? "She loves the theater, travel, and spending time with me," noted Jesse. He arranged to extend a New York business trip an extra day, bought Broadway tickets, and invited his mother. "She was thrilled, warmed up fast, dropped the chill," reported a relieved Jesse. He had sent a convincing message of affection for his mother, while at the same time spurning destructive family habits of underresponsibility and overresponsibility.

6. **Give the shift time.** For several months Jesse's mother called with "emergency" rescue requests, ignoring his revised rescue guidelines. "It's just a new fan belt. Can't you fix that?" she'd plead. "Mechanically challenged, Mom. Can't do the fan belt." Another day: "You said you could paint, and my cousin comes in two days. Can you take a day off work and paint today?" "I can paint after six," offered Jesse. He gently

repelled his mother's subtle and not-so-subtle efforts to prod him back into dysfunctional family traditions, patiently letting the message seep in that the old Jesse was gone for good.

7. **Expect changes in other members of your family as well.** Jesse's mother now had to organize her requests with respect to his schedule and assume greater responsibility for herself. As she gained confidence in her own competence, she began to expect more adult responsibility of her live-in sons as well. She became unwilling to relieve them of all laundry, meal, and household duties, partly because she could no longer unload their underresponsibility onto Jesse. As a result, one son chose to move out once Mom resigned as the free maid, cook, and butler.

Relational shifts take time to succeed, but within a year this mother and her three adult sons had assumed more mature roles, noticed diminishing tension, and felt greater mutual respect—all because Jesse had chosen to stop the cycle and free himself from unhealthy habits. Blocked from old habits of imposition and exploitation, Jesse's mother and her cherished son learned to treat each other with greater consideration. Jesse rebuffed arbitrarily imposed roles, and his carefully calibrated behavior changes triggered a shift throughout the entire family system. Executed with generous doses of sensitivity, courage, and resolve, this liberation formula offered win-win results as Jesse and his family matured into more balanced relationships.

THE PARADOX OF THE "VICTIM" CONSPIRATOR

Emotionally paralyzed by fear of offending his beloved mother, Jesse nevertheless blamed her for her excessive dependence that put him at risk. But his own collusion enabled her behaviors, as is common not only in families but in relationships generally. If he was exploited, it was only possible with his cooperation, making him a self-saboteur. So it goes with imposed family roles: At some level they are often self-inflicted.

Because Jesse and his mother had deep affection for one another, they were able to identify and purge self-sabotaging behaviors in their family. But affection is often the *last* feeling expressed when I challenge crisis-rattled clients to revise their own toxic roles in the family. Cheryl was one whose rage had vaporized any warm fuzzy feelings for her husband, Stephen.

> WHEN WE ARE EXPLOITED, IT IS OFTEN WITH OUR COOPERATION, MAKING US SELF-SABOTEURS.

"Explain why we're here," demanded fiery-eyed Cheryl to her mate of fifteen years, as both sat on a sofa in my office.

"I had an affair," mumbled Stephen.

"With whom?" she snapped.

"With a masseuse," he answered.

"How'd you know this masseuse?" she prodded.

"You sent me to her for my back," he explained, eyes cast to the floor.

Cheryl oozed contempt while Stephen shrank into a guilt-laden heap, agreeing that he had ravaged the marriage. For sure, the affair had inflicted deep emotional wounds. But I wondered if there were injuries from *before* the infidelity that were also causing the relationship to bleed to death.

"Was this affair an *exit* from the marital relationship?" I inquired.

"No, I want to save the marriage," Stephen responded.

"You bet it was an exit!" countered Cheryl. "After three children I'm not ready to give up. But I'd sure call this an exit!"

"All relationships have exits, some overt, some covert, some minor, some major. The question is: What exits have shaped this relationship other than the covert but dramatic choice of an affair?"

Eyeing the chart below, Cheryl's demeanor softened:

RELATIONSHIP EXITS

OVERT	COVERT
Open affair	Secret affair
Separation	Work
Divorce	Children
Hostility	Extended family
Abuse	Friends
	Church
	TV
	Hobbies
	Emotional distance

Using this self-scrutiny tool, Cheryl identified her demanding job and three children as factors that had siphoned most of her attention away from Stephen. Now that she thought about it, yes, she viewed these influences as subconscious evasions of emotional intimacy with her husband.

An unexpressive sort, Stephen was harder to read on the exit issue, other than his affair. But slowly, old resentments bubbled to the surface—such as their house being next door to Cheryl's aunt. Stephen disliked both the house and the aunt, but Cheryl had been determined to move next to her aunt (who was also her best friend).

Then there was his job. Although the job paid well, it had been engineered through the aunt's impressive connections. Stephen loathed the position. "At times," he noted, "it's more like Cheryl and her aunt are married and I'm the outsider."

"Are you saying that Cheryl's tight bond with her aunt makes you feel as if you're on the outside of key marital and family decisions?"

"Exactly," said Stephen.

Cheryl was pensive, and I could almost see the lightbulbs popping on in her mind. "My aunt and I have endured a long, painful family history and I discuss everything with her. I don't deny that she has enormous influence over me," Cheryl confided.

"Is it valid to consider this a type of exit from your marital relationship?"

"It wasn't intentional, but probably this is a fair observation," responded a very sober Cheryl.

"So looking at these detours from emotional intimacy—affair, children, work, aunt—which exits came first?"

"My exits," answered Cheryl as Stephen sat in silence.

By leaving Stephen emotionally through other commitments, Cheryl had pushed this husband and father into an outsider role in his own home. By capitulating to Cheryl's demands, Stephen passively reinforced Cheryl's role as a family czar wielding iron rule.

As Stephen and Cheryl accepted more mutual accountability, hope for a restored relationship grew. But Stephen still had to face some hard facts about his own slow slide into marital treachery.

"Stephen, who, by threat of death, coerced you into that house or job you resent so?"

More silence, as Stephen was deep in thought. "Nobody. I hate confrontation and I knew both Cheryl and her aunt would be mad if I balked. It was easier to go along," he finally answered.

"So who were you protecting by capitulation?"

Recalculating his motives, Stephen paused. "Myself. I'd have to say I was protecting myself," he responded.

Within minutes, perceptions shifted as Stephen and Cheryl reexamined the marital wounds they had inflicted on one another, often unconsciously. Cheryl was outraged at Stephen for having an affair. But she admitted that she had pursued numerous exits from the marriage long before Stephen did. She set the stage for a wrenching marital drama. But Stephen alone bore responsibility for the choices he made on that stage.

Stephen resented his minimized roles as husband and father due to Cheryl's emotionally fused relationship with her aunt. Yet he *chose* to shrivel in stature through meek capitulation to others' demands. Through passivity, Stephen denied his family a husband and father guided by integrity and good judgment.

Throughout their early marriage, Cheryl was no Miss Congeniality and Stephen was no profile in courage. Together they both chose roles that undermined the partnership they both claimed to cherish.

Through a liberation process similar to Jesse's, Cheryl and Stephen were able to shed the destructive roles they had imposed on each other. Regretting the pain his affair had caused Cheryl, Stephen assumed greater responsibility for an authentic relationship. He truthfully expressed his desires and opinions rather than allowing his fear of confrontation to neutralize him. He made it clear that in the future he would refuse to passively agree to marital or family decisions injected by outsiders.

Those who plan what is good find love and faithfulness.

PROVERBS 14:22

Remorseful for her more subtle ways of abandoning Stephen, Cheryl set clearer boundaries with her aunt. She also reorganized work and child schedules to assure quality time with Stephen, so they could nurture each other and care for their marriage.

MENTAL AND MORAL TUNE-UPS

Jesse and his mother, as well as Cheryl and Stephen, were doomed to relational misery until they agreed to mental and moral realignment.

Mental recalibration

On the mental front, they were all victims of fuzzy thinking that fueled emotional and relational turmoil. In *The Feeling Good Handbook*, best-selling author David Burns, MD, offers

STRATEGIC QUESTIONS FOR REVISED FAMILY ROLES

When you're annoyed and frustrated by family roles, answering a few questions can help guide a liberation strategy beneficial to all parties:

1. What role have you served in your family of origin? Possibilities include hero, rescuer, overresponsible one, overdependent one, scapegoat, helpless one, mascot-clown, surrogate parent, surrogate spouse.

2. Who assigned you your role? How did they impose your role? How do you continue that role now—in your family of origin, in your current household, or in social and work relationships?

3. What benefits do you gain from your role? How do your behaviors protect relationships, avoid conflict, or preserve opportunities?

4. What risks are posed by your role? Does your behavior perpetuate childlike dependence on others? stall maturation for other passive adults? contribute to financial crippling, social isolation, or other emotional, relational, or social costs?

5. Who *benefits* from your role? How?

6. What family members are *harmed* by your role—possibly by their own stalled maturation and squelched competence?

7. Who in this family functions as your *bridge* to others in or outside the family? Who functions as a *wall* between you and others? Which relatives are a *wall* between you and opportunity? Who functions as a *bomb* in your relations with others or in life generally?

8. For whom in your family do *you* serve as a bridge (in their relations to others or access to opportunity)? a wall? a bomb?

9. What roles would be healthier for you? What behaviors must you change to shift into these healthier roles?

step-by-step guidance for controlling relationship-wrecking cognitive distortions.[2] A number are illustrated here.

- **Emotional reasoning:** Since he felt shame, Jesse assumed it was shameful if he failed to respond to all his mother's demands. This mother-son relationship grew much stronger once Jesse realized that feelings do not always reflect truth, and that "honoring" a parent cannot require controlling another adult's happiness, because that is mission impossible.
- **All-or-nothing thinking:** Jesse's mom believed that if he loved her he would do all she asked. She was able to avoid feelings of rejection when she accepted his right to choose some ways to help her, while declining other demands.
- **Mental filter:** Jesse's mother minimized his positive responses to her but obsessed about negatives, which made her depressed. Learning to recognize both the joy of connection when Jesse was with her and the disappointment she felt when Jesse was less available gave his mother a more accurate perspective and greater emotional stability.
- **"Should" expectations:** Cheryl decided when Stephen "should" do this and "should" do that, assuring blame if he exercised his own judgment. Their marriage gained new hope when Cheryl respected Stephen's right to choose goals that might veer from her agenda.
- **Jumping to conclusions:** Stephen assumed he'd pay a higher price for standing up to Cheryl than for

capitulating, but the whole family paid tragically for his spaghetti-spined approach to marriage. When he became more guided by principles than by fear of his wife's anger, he was happier with his marriage and Cheryl respected him more.

Moral recalibration

These families were also crippled by moral laziness reflected by excessive need for approval, childish dependence, a sense of entitlement to superior treatment, and mindless conformity to others' demands. They summoned courage for the new moral choices described below. Which choices could improve relations in your own family?

- **Integrity trumps approval:** Stephen knew that capitulation to Cheryl was destructive to his marriage and his family, but he was willing to betray his beliefs to gain approval. When he decided integrity meant more than seeking approval, his marriage began to mend.
- **Responsibility—not childish dependence:** Jesse's mom sought affection through clinging dependence on her son. The mother finally graduated to an adult role when she embraced reasonable responsibility for her own well-being.
- **Accountability—not entitlement:** Cheryl exuded an entitlement mentality, assuming that Stephen owed it to her to give her cherished aunt influence over family decisions, to buy a house he disliked, and in many other ways to accept misery so she could be happy. As Cheryl and Stephen accepted mutual accountability, respond-

ing to each other's questions, doubts, or disagreement, they ended a form of family tyranny by embracing "justice for all" in the household.

- **Volition—not mindless capitulation:** As Stephen learned, it was not enough to know the right choices. As Jesse learned, it was not enough to have good intentions. Stephen needed the courage to act on convictions and Jesse needed clearer thinking about loving choices for himself and his mother. Relational relief came when Stephen and Jesse gained volition—a will strong enough to execute wise plans.

Clarity. Integrity. Courage. Resolve. A bit of sensitivity. That blend of ingredients brought Jesse and his mom, and Cheryl and Stephen, *home again*. Home to the other's heart, made safe. Home to the other's mind, made open. Home to chosen, not imposed, roles.

You and your family can take the same journey—*home again*.

PLAN FOR TRANSFORMATION

- **Adopt a chosen role, not an imposed role**
- **Inform your family members of roles and behaviors you choose**
- **Expect anger**
- **Avoid blame or defensiveness**
- **Initiate affirming contact with the angry party**
- **Give the shift time**
- **Expect changes in other members of your family as well**

TRANSFORMING HABIT
Minimize the family tyrant's power over you.

SIX

TAMING FAMILY TYRANTS

She challenged a U.S. president and brought him down, but not before he and his people threatened physical assault as well as professional and financial annihilation.

Her intent was not to manipulate political machinery but to out the truth. Ultimately, it was truth—not *Washington Post* publisher Katharine Graham—that sent a brilliant but imprudent Richard Nixon careening into history.

Through the legal, journalistic, social, and political chaos of Watergate, Katharine Graham, seemingly hard as nails, stood resolute.

Who but her intimates would suspect that Katharine Graham commandeered a slice of American history after years of excruciating oppression by a tyrannical spouse?

She had shared only a few social events with Phil Graham

when he proposed. "I was charmed and dazzled," Katharine reported in her 1997 autobiography. "And I was incredulous—this brilliant, charismatic, fascinating man loved me!"[1]

He came from a difficult life with his poor Florida family, but as president of the *Harvard Law Review* Phil Graham solidified jet-setting social connections. With some reluctance, he accepted an offer to move into top management of the *Washington Post,* which was owned by Katharine's father. Named publisher just shy of his thirty-first birthday, the charismatic Graham captured the attention of heads of state and international corporate and media elite.

At home, Katharine practically volunteered to be the victim of a darker side of Phil Graham. "Perversely, I had seemed to enjoy the role of doormat wife. For whatever reason, I liked to be dominated," Katharine wrote much later. "Thoroughly fascinated and charmed by Phil, I was also slightly resentful . . . feeling such complete dependence on another person."[2]

The Grahams fit a family profile described by Dr. Susan Forward in *Emotional Blackmail,* where victims often subconsciously encourage their own psychological battering through behaviors that reward, perpetuate, or fail to impede abuse.[3]

A marital pattern developed of violent quarrels often fueled by alcohol, then apologies and diminished drinking. As Katharine described, "The fights were never in public—the rage would explode after we had left a place and was usually about nothing substantive. . . . He seemed to seize on something as an excuse to vent his rage."[4]

BULLY CONTROLLER TACTICS

While Graham sought Katharine's constant companionship and encouraged her intellectual and professional growth, he verbally assaulted her regularly and made her the subject of cruel humor and the butt of family jokes.

Such hostile attacks "gradually undermined my self-confidence almost entirely," wrote Katharine, but "I was still so mesmerized by him that I didn't perceive what was happening."[5]

In time, Katharine's private misery went public. Phil Graham's repeated bouts with debilitating depression overlapped an ostentatious affair, bizarre public behavior, and impulsive exorbitant buying sprees.

When Phil announced he not only planned to marry his mistress but also to keep the *Washington Post* controlling shares given by his father-in-law, Katharine finally dug in her heels. Leave her he might—but not with the family legacy.

Those who habitually inflict emotional and psychological violence on others, notes Patricia Evans in *The Verbally Abusive Relationship*, tend to expect a free pass.[6] Phil Graham was in for a shock.

Katharine won the battle to rescue the *Post*. She also determined to protect herself from abusive behaviors. Phil Graham was fortunate that after months of transatlantic flings with his mistress, his wife accepted him back into her life and into their home. He brought with him a scary diagnosis that explained much of his behavior: manic depression, today known as bipolar disorder.

A condition that could have been managed somewhat

through quality care had by now left Graham despondent. He soon ended a promising but turbulent life with a self-inflicted gunshot wound.

Though traumatized, Katharine Graham was fortunate in many ways. Thanks to her family's wealth, financial security for herself and her four children was never an issue. As time would reveal, she was also loaded with the same genes that had transformed her family into an American media powerhouse.

Even while Phil was alive and Katharine fought for the family business, she was surrounded by people who believed deeply in her ability to take over the helm of the *Post*. Moreover, she was shielded by a cadre of gifted and dedicated corporate officers and journalists. Long crushed by forces beyond her control, Katharine Graham had learned to harness external power constructively.

When Katharine Graham later took on some of the globe's greatest human powers during Watergate, she demonstrated capacity for remarkable independence, courage, and resolve. But as is true for many people, her personal life was riddled

---

EXTERNAL DECISION-MAKING FACTORS

(May Also Be Used As *Controller Compliance Tools*)

Coercion	by those who hold power of punishment
Reward	by those who control tangible and intangible resources
Expertise	by those believed to have superior skill
Charisma	by those whose appealing personality can squelch others' independence
Authority	by those wielding earned or assigned power
Knowledge	by those perceived as wiser, smarter, or more informed

with sorrow as long as she yielded to abusive external controls, as noted in the chart on page 76.

CYCLES OF TYRANNY

Phil Graham's mood swings—from charming to abusive then back to a more mellow state—are common in cyclical abusers. As Katharine Graham discovered, those who live with cyclical abusers degenerate into human tennis balls: *Wham!* They're whacked in one direction, then *slam!* back in the other.

First, the abuser accommodates in ways that seduce others into emotional, social, and physical quicksand. Then, rising tension sends ripples of turbulence—sometimes *exclusively* to intimate partners.

Next comes an explosion of venomous verbal attacks or a burst of violence. If fueled by mind- and emotion-curdling alcohol or drugs, the eruptions can be more frequent and molten. Finally, the abuser retreats into an illusion of tranquility, even remorse, often luring victims back into the snare.

Limit your exposure to angry personalities. Their toxic emotions are contagious and they are treacherous to your soul.

DERIVED FROM PROVERBS 22:24-25

Research shows that family abusers often have the traits of borderline personality disorder. This breed is hypervigilant, incessantly scanning for treachery, often finding it where it doesn't exist. Their warped social radar produces vacillating, unreliable trust, and such personalities are repeatedly burnt as they mistrust reliable allies and instead put their trust in the treacherous.

Phil Graham's confused mind led to the same pattern, as he unleashed vicious verbal assaults not only on a committed spouse, but also on loyal colleagues and even on President John F. Kennedy, who had befriended him. It was Graham's in-your-face, confrontational, inflammatory attacks, not his imagined adversaries, that put his career, family, and fortune at risk.

Obsessed with wanting to control everything and everyone in their environment, typical tough-talking bullies tend to have a confused self-concept, personal emptiness, chronic depression, and an inability to soothe or calm themselves. As relationship addicts, they desperately seek to derive a sense of their own value from others and are tormented by conflicting terrors:

- That they may be abandoned by loves or allies
- That they will be smothered by close relationships that could dilute control

Cling, panic, reject. Cling, panic, reject. Such is the cycle common to the bully controller. It is no wonder such abusers are chronically agonized by dead-end relationships, social isolation, and squashed social support.

John N. Briere, a professor at the University of Southern California School of Medicine, has found a strong link between such borderline-abuser traits and early childhood emotional and physical anguish.[7]

Despite stereotypes of mothers as chief child-shapers,

researchers note that a father's rejection is most likely to transform a precious son into a domestic terrorist for his future wife, children, and society.

As reported in *The Abusive Personality* by Donald G. Dutton, the biggest childhood contributors to adult abusiveness in order of importance include:

1. Father rejection felt by child
2. Father coldness felt by child
3. Father physical abuse
4. Father verbal abuse
5. Mother rejection felt by child

Clearly, abuse is not limited to the physical. Physical abuse assaults the body, but it is the "corrosive attack on the boy's sense of self" through public humiliation, random punishment, and verbal attacks on the personality, notes Dutton, that most predicts a future emotional or physical abuser.

"If I had to pick one single action by the parent that generated abusiveness in men," concludes this University of British Columbia professor of psychology, "I would pick being shamed by the father."[8]

About the resilient, we are still left with the mystery of how people who are tripped, trapped, hit, hated or left can . . . rise, over time, phoenixlike from the ashes.

GINA O'CONNELL HIGGINS,
Resilient Adults: Overcoming a Cruel Past

Adults traumatized in childhood often have a warped neu-
ral structure that jolts into overreaction at the slightest hint of
risk. Like a post-traumatic stress disorder victim, a child who
has been abused or neglected by his parents may bury a volatile mix of rage, shame, mistrust, and anxiety. Once that child
becomes an adult, what is buried often erupts. Neither the
adult-victim nor a romantic partner—a new intimate figure
who replaces the parents—foresees the volcano that can blow.

After a few eruptions, "the abusiveness is hardwired into
the system. They are programmed for intimate violence," says
Dutton.[9] The victim is now the violator, and deeply buried
abuse tendencies will rigidly resist change. When such rela-
tionship-annihilating behavior is directed exclusively at the
intimate partner, outsiders never observe the abuser's Jekyll
and Hyde nature.

The victim in such cases may be viewed as a whiner, ingrate,
or nut when she (most often) complains of a spouse whom others see only as a gentleman or, at the very worst, harmless. Survivor skills include learning to constructively harness the very
external decision-making factors (see page 76) that the abuser
uses for destruction. Katharine Graham exercised such external power by winning allies whose expertise, knowledge, and
authority helped her prevail in legal and corporate battles to
retain her family heirloom, the *Washington Post*.

LOW-GRADE CONTROLLERS

Your own family tyrant may offer less drama than Phil
Graham, but low-grade family controllers, like low-grade ura-
nium, still radiate risk. In many of my Family Habits work-

shops, participants have offered their own stories for group consideration. Consider the following family-controller stories for yourself, as well as possible responses. What would *you* do if you faced such family-controller situations?

- **Clean Machine.** Annette's parents demand that she drive seventy-five miles each way to wash their van every month. The car wash in their little town is "cheap and quite good," reports Annette, but her parents say no one makes the car sparkle like Annette. They won't visit with her or have her in the house when she comes—they just want that van cleaned! She gets the silent treatment if she doesn't comply.

- **Time's Up.** Cherie's husband demands dinner every night at 6:00 PM sharp, regardless of the fact that she must also serve as chauffeur for five children with complicated soccer-basketball-swim team-birthday party schedules. If dinner slips to 6:10 PM, Cherie can count on a sullen Gerald who will then sleep in the guest room.

- **Moocher Heaven.** Thirty-year-old Albert, his wife, and three kids moved into his widowed mother's basement for a month. They soon took over the whole house and expected Grandma to fix all their meals, pay for everything, and pick up their clutter . . . as the month dragged into a year. A very exasperated Grandma has no idea how to unload the moochers without alienating her only son.

- **Hot Monogamy.** If Glenn awakens at two o'clock in

the morning and he's in the mood, he gives Frances a poke, then a big nudge—expecting hot monogamy on demand. *It's not much to expect,* he thinks, *since I earn all the money.*

- **Designing Women.** A very excited Gay was waiting until closer to her wedding date to order an exact fit of her dream wedding gown. Meanwhile, her mother secretly hired a seamstress to make a duplicate of *her* twenty-five-year-old gown—a style unflattering to a daughter with a very different figure. The fifty-year-old mom is outraged at Gay's ingratitude.

- **What Nuts!** Kevin moved into the townhouse of his bride, Gloria. Having a passion for chilled peanut butter, he stuck a jar in the fridge. The next day, he found it on the counter, all warmed up. Back it went into the fridge. Out it came again onto the counter, this time with a note: *Kevin—Keep this peanut butter in the pantry where it belongs!* Okay, so he had odd taste. But he was also ordered absolutely *not* to hang coats in the front closet; absolutely *not* to waste freezer space with more than one type of ice cream; and absolutely *not* to run up the electric bill with more than one light on in a room. This was *Gloria's* house, and no mere husband was going to botch her system!

■　■　■

Locked into a theater of the absurd, targets of such family domination feel stressed, diminished, and demoralized. What to do?

With a story fit for *Prime Time Live,* Abigail demonstrated a shrewd strategy for deflecting the family controller. Her tale comes straight out of 1 Samuel 25—one reason Abigail resonates deeply during my Family Habits workshops based in churches. In a nation where Gallup polls report that 95 percent of the population believe in God and 65 percent claim church membership, Abigail's story has much relevance for victims of twenty-first-century family oppression.[10]

Abigail's impulsive, boozing husband, Nabal, made the fatal mistake of picking a fight with David, a guy who quickly rounded up a four-hundred-man posse bent on vigilante justice. They vowed to slaughter not only Nabal, but also every male on his ranch, no questions asked.

Nabal was like today's substance abusers, who not only injure families directly but also generate grim indirect treachery. When such abusers are male, spouses and children must shoulder husband and father responsibilities, as it's too risky to rely on the erratic, unpredictable, sometimes volatile substance abuser. The family reputation is left in tatters by the abuser's irresponsible behaviors, with spouses and children humiliated and ostracized. Antisocial behaviors also provoke punitive action by court systems and law enforcement agencies, just as Nabal incited vigilante action not just against himself but also against his extended household. The abuser's indirect assaults on the family violate and control them emotionally, spiritually, physically, financially, and socially, leaving invisible but debilitating wounds that can fester for generations.

On high alert for such peril from Nabal, panicked ranch hands warned Abigail, who had the vision to see both danger and opportunity. A strategic thinker, she avoided one and seized the other. She bolstered her success by savvy use of external assets: wise counsel from subordinates, worthy allies, and favorable circumstances—a distracted Nabal and a ready cache of peace offerings.

A prudent person foresees danger and takes precautions.
The simpleton goes blindly on and suffers the consequences.

PROVERBS 22:3, NLT

Strong willed but diplomatic, Abigail successfully negotiated with a homicidal David, the future king of Israel, who had rashly led his vigilantes into a battle of revenge. As for drunken Nabal, when he was finally detoxed enough to get it, he was terrified. He'd come very close to checking out—involuntarily. The prospect of wilderness justice vaporized his belligerent, menacing, cocky inner core—*whoosh!*—just that fast.

THE NEED FOR INTERNAL DIRECTION

In the land of the patriarchs, why would a group of male ranch hands targeted for massacre turn to a *woman* for help?

Abigail had a stockpile of internal assets that made her a stealthy and powerful defensive weapon. Such internal decision-making tools predict a person's impact on family and surrounding society.

It's not just that Abigail came equipped with stellar inner radar. This woman of faith was propelled by the sort of purpose-driven life described in Rick Warren's *New York Times* best

---

INTERNAL DECISION-MAKING FACTORS

Will	Inner resolve related to volition, autonomy, self-determination
Knowledge	Facts, research, objective data
Vision	View of goals and strategy for reaching them
Judgment	Decision making based on data, instincts
Conscience	Inner direction based on right and wrong
Social Radar	Instinctive understanding of behavior and attitudes and of their impact on other people
Faith	Reliance on God for direction, protection, and eternal significance and security

---

seller of that title.[11] Her God-focused agenda and potent conscience would not allow her to put her own security above those targeted by David's revenge. But Abigail also knew that David's core values were in sync with her own, assuming she could penetrate his rage.

"David passionately desired to know God above all else. . . . He craved God," observes Rick Warren.[12] The intuitive Abigail warned David that bloody revenge would sabotage his deepest longing: to be closer to his God.

David's exhale nearly ripples from the text.

Israel's heroic, handsome, dashing, poetic, passionate, and now-awed future king was dazzled by this clearheaded, bold, daring woman. When Nabal dropped dead just ten days after his self-inflicted trauma, David, attracted by Abigail's wisdom and courage, entreated her to be *his* wife.

Take a look at the case studies in the appendix, starting on page 161. These studies may help you evaluate ways in which internal radar—like Abigail's—is essential if you wish to take back your life from a pathological family controller.

Controller deflection

Responses to family controllers tend to come in two extremes: capitulation or retaliation.

Passively allowing another person to control our life, as if he or she were God, says C. S. Lewis, is an act of idolatry. But harsh or vindictive responses are also treacherous, turning wounded victims into new abusers. As Abigail proved, the best tactics for controller deflection involve self-control and good judgment. The controller-deflection principles (see next page) are critical in disarming the controller in your life.

DEATH TALK VS. LIFE TALK

"Come closer," rasped the voice from the hospital pillow. On guard against a mother prone to erupt with spirit-shriveling verbal assaults, Geraldine tentatively moved closer to her mother, Marilyn. The doctors predicted she would not live beyond the next twenty-four hours. "I will speak to you from the grave," whispered Marilyn, with lips curled in a slight smile but her eyes cold as steel.

Geraldine shivered. Her mother typically delivered on inevitably sinister vows, and Geraldine expected this would be no exception.

Soft earth was barely settling over Marilyn's grave when her attorney contacted her two daughters and three grandchildren for the reading of her will. Marilyn had been a socially prominent matron of substantial means, so the will could dramatically alter the life of her five presumptive heirs.

And so it did. All five children and grandchildren were named in the will. Four were bequeathed small household ob-

---

CONTROLLER-DEFLECTION PRINCIPLES

- Exercise conscience, judgment, and will rather than capitulate to coercive or exploitative external controls.

- Honor others' rights to choose for themselves—but not for you.

- Speak candidly without assaulting, blaming, or whining: *You're talking to others made in God's image too. Handle with care.*

- Choose options conducive to mature functioning of all parties.

- Avoid options that perpetuate controlling behaviors—by yourself or others.

- As much as possible, choose actions that preserve integrity while protecting desirable relationships.

- Consider using the Family Freedom Formula. (See page 59.)

---

jects, prompting their new owners to feel once again the reproach of a voice that even in death would not be silenced. The fifth heir, Geraldine's son, was Marilyn's sole financial beneficiary. Not that he was ever given his grandmother's consideration, care, or courtesy in life. But now he served as a useful tool of torment, a human lever to ratchet up emotional pain.

This grandson received a trust exceeding $1.5 million. Controlled by trustees, the trust could be used to sustain or improve his vehicles and household property or even pay his mortgage payments. But the terms assured that such payments covered only vehicles registered in his name and kept on his property or goods moved into or improving his family residence. If such terms were broken, trust benefits would shift to a charity named by the deceased, and her carefully chosen trustees were unlikely to tolerate deviation from these limitations.

Numbed to the lifelong mental, emotional, and physical insults of their mother, Geraldine and her sister had anticipated more of the same through the will and thus had prepared to be disinherited. They anticipated the grandchildren were likely to be as well. But equality of scorn would have been too simple for the scheming matriarch of this family. By favoring one grandson with benefits he was unlikely to refuse and unable to share, from the grave she choreographed a dance of despair, resentment, and bitterness engulfing every member of her extended family.

What are the roots of a personality that is so malevolent and narcissistic, so totally devoted to personal indulgence and comfort, regardless of pain inflicted on others? In *Restructuring Personality Disorders,* Dr. Jeffrey J. Magnavita says that the number one factor in producing a narcissist is parenting a child as if he or she were special, superior to others and deserving better treatment.[13]

Arrogant with a grossly inflated ego, narcissists at their core are so insecure that they can actually feel impoverished by efforts to give or love, says Dr. Judith Mishne, New York University social work professor.[14]

Marilyn, like many family destroyers, had the traits of a narcissist. The objectives, tactics, and outcomes of their schemes can feel cold as death, clouding the mind and crippling relationships. The destroyer is exposed by "death talk" that is deadly effective in wounding and destroying, while lacking the restraint and care of "life talk" that seeks to heal wounds, reduce risk, and assure emotional security for all parties.

Consider the contrasting goals (both conscious or subconscious) of destructive and constructive personalities in the chart on the next page.

Particularly mind-twisting are destroyers who wield death-talk tactics and then show shock or resentment when they fail to achieve life-talk rewards! How many marital partners daily assault their spouse with heart-pulverizing insults and threats before unleashing more blame when their sexual initiatives are spurned? Think of the logic here: *You're the sick one if I can't brutalize you into a romantic mood!*

These same people batter children with contempt, rejection, and sabotage for years, then accuse their teenagers of disrespect, ingratitude, and rebellion when they fail to exhibit ample reverence. The message from the elder is: *After I pulverize your spirit, vaporize your self-esteem, and cripple your social skills, you must demonstrate clear respect for my character, deference to my status, and responsiveness to my wise counsel.* The destroyer skillfully digs original wounds ever deeper.

What a price their victims pay. Children who are devalued and emotionally abandoned by their family have higher rates of chronic depression, deflated self-esteem, and crippling indecisiveness. They tend to seek constant validation of personal worth but are too terrified of rejection to stand up for themselves. They lurch between extremes: from isolating behaviors to instant intimacy; from suspicion to treacherous trust; and from idealization to demonization of others. When fully grown they still suffer from malevolently narcissistic parents who do not willingly give up abusive and controlling behaviors just because their children have become adults. No

COMMUNICATION GOALS, TACTICS, AND OUTCOMES

Death-Talk Goals
- Control of victim
- Revenge—emotional and physical pain
- Manipulation
- Entitlement
- Confusion
- Power
- Coerced identity and roles
- Annihilation of victim

Death-Talk Tactics and Tools
- Uncontrolled rage
- Verbal and emotional assault
- Exhaustive accusations and demands
- Rigid blame
- Intimidation and emotional blackmail
- "Hit and run"

Death Talk's Impact on Others
- Emotional deadness
- Numbness to pain—his own and others'
- Deafness to destroyer
- Fragmented personality—lurching from guilt to rage to self-pity to hatred of destroyer and self
- Social alienation and crippling
- Abuse—physical and verbal
- Intimacy capacity diminished or demolished
- Pessimism
- Hopelessness

Life-Talk Goals
- Emotional intimacy
- Mutual safety—emotional and physical
- Reciprocal influence and responsiveness
- Shared responsibility
- Understanding
- Integrity

- Authenticity
- Preservation of self and other

Life-Talk Tactics and Tools
- Restrained anger and speech
- Judicious communication
- Selective critiques and requests
- Objectivity: shared blame
- Diplomacy and peace compacts
- Paced examination of issues

Life Talk's Impact on Others
- Emotional security
- Empathy and compassion for others
- Openness to others' hurts and wounds
- Resilient personality—balancing joy with sorrow, self-care with generosity, ambition with altruism
- Social connectedness and empowerment
- Resistance to victimization
- Intimacy capacity enhanced and maximized
- Optimism
- Hope

wonder these wounded hearts are repeatedly stung by dead-end relationships.

There *are* ways to constructively break a family legacy of tyranny. As Stephanie Donaldson-Pressman and Robert M. Pressman explain in *The Narcissistic Family: Diagnosis and Treatment,* adult children of destroyers must start with courageous and objective assessment of their family of origin. They must mourn losses inflicted by childhood neglect and abuse. They must examine ongoing fallout. And they must take responsibility for change.[15]

In Nehemiah chapter 9, this ancient Hebrew sage outlined the process of moving on from traumatic family history. Whether in Nehemiah's day or now, chaos in the family

---

NEHEMIAH'S FAMILY-LEGACY RECOVERY FORMULA

1. Confess sins of fathers: Acknowledge historic family wounds

2. Assess impact of family failure: Make clear value judgments and assign responsibility

3. Chronicle overlooked or underrated family heroes, victories, and achievements—often disregarded or downgraded as victims wallow in family pain

4. Lean heavily on personal responsibility and divine guidance for an escape hatch from chronic and debilitating family habits

---

presents painful choices. One option is to ignore family destroyers and the trauma they produce, refusing to admit past destruction or to confront current tyranny. A new generation is then sacrificed as family destroyers leave more crippled lives in their wake.

The second option—breaking the cycle and identifying the destroyers in your family—may require enormous courage, but it's crucial for healing. Ironically, family bullies who have unleashed years or even decades of havoc with impunity sometimes respond with remarkable compliance when confronted with moral courage.

THE DESTROYER SOULPRINT

Just as every human exhibits a unique thumbprint, so we all display distinct "soulprints" along life's course. Our words, attitudes, values, and behaviors etch indelible imprints on the mind and heart of those who cohabit our life space. The signature soulprint of a family destroyer is that of a malicious narcissist who goes beyond mere self-absorption and seems to want to wound, confuse, disable, and annihilate his or her victims. Consider the destroyer traits listed on the next page as illustrated by the cases in this book.

The Israelites . . . confessed their sins and the wickedness of their fathers. NEHEMIAH 9:1-2

INOCULATION FROM FAMILY DESTROYERS

How is it possible to escape the clutches of family destroyers? As Katharine Graham and Abigail demonstrated, it is possible to resist destructive family habits. But the decision to break the cycle carries a price. The questions you must ask yourself are these:

- What could your liberation plan cost you emotionally, socially, financially, and otherwise?
- Are you willing to pay that price?
- What price will you pay if you refuse to resist a chronic destroyer?

Once you realize the importance of breaking the cycle, you can begin by building a protective shield to guard against the assaults of your family tyrant.

1. **Launch liberation in your mind.** Katharine Graham's capitulation to spousal emotional abuse could have continued indefinitely as long as she believed that she

DESTROYER TRAITS

Destroyer Mind-Set and Habits	Examples
Entitlement Mentality	As if whacking a wrecking ball against her marriages, pampered Christine (chapter 4) seemed to expect her husbands to cater to her whims the way her parents had. Each one bolted from Christine's attitude of entitlement.
Inflated Self-Importance/ Arrogance	Matriarch Marilyn (chapter 6) used the status of wealth and advantage of her age to impose unearned power over her extended family.
Deadened Conscience/Moral Blindness/ Corroded Emotions	While exuding self-righteousness, the Bible-quoting deacon dad of Bonnie, Bryan, and Bobby (chapters 1 and 2) seemed oblivious to the emotional, physical, and spiritual violence he inflicted on his children.
Chronic, Extreme, and Often Exhibitionist Rage	Known to his family and employees for his molten rage, Nabal (chapter 6) risked many lives when his antagonism against the heroic David exploded into a public forum.
Demands Unmerited Favor and Respect	Destroyers cited here indulged in childish tantrums, but they were outraged and resentful when not treated with the utmost respect, as if they had behaved as a mature and honorable family elder.
Manipulation and Exploitation	Ben Carson's charming father deceived and manipulated a trusting young woman, who was left to raise her sons in poverty when their father's bigamy was exposed (chapter 8).
Vindictive Schemes	Retaliating through her will for their failure to exhibit the adoration and servitude she demanded, Matriarch Marilyn discounted her family's gracious endurance during decades of her abuse.

was terminally inferior and subservient. As in her case, abdication of adult decision making is no way to prove love and loyalty.

2. **Purge distorted aspects of your identity** that have been imposed by destroyers. Abraham Lincoln's own liberation began when he mentally expunged messages from his father that he deserved emotional and physical abuse and that he was unworthy of education or aspirations for achievement. (See chapter 2.) Abe soaked up affirmation from others and disproved his father's bleak assessment of a son who was, in fact, remarkable.

3. **Refuse to accept a victim identity.** Obsessing about her neglectful parents nearly locked Sharon into chronic victim status—while at the same time perpetuating their control over her existence. (See chapter 4.) Sharon rejected the habit of victimhood, assuming more responsibility for her life and destiny. In doing so, she stripped family controllers of power over her.

4. **Infuse positive identity factors.** *Strong, resilient, courageous, spirited,* and *faithful* were terms used by friends and colleagues to describe Bonnie. (See chapter 2.) Like a parched sponge, she soaked up and savored the praise and affirmation she received from those outside her family. As she tapped these positive traits, Bonnie was able to repel her father's efforts to impose a dehumanizing identity on her life.

5. **Anticipate the threats, anger, scorn, and possible retaliation of family tyrants.** Because of Phil's life

habits, Katharine Graham was able to predict and prepare mentally for his reactionary rage as she moved toward constructive decision making. He lost the ambush advantage.

6. **Calculate the price you can tolerate for emancipation** and pay that price mentally before it's coerced. Bodybuilder Jesse (see chapter 5) assumed that deviation from his mother's risky demands could stir anger and rejection. By anticipating that possibility, he became immune to emotional blackmail and her pressure to capitulate.

7. **Limit and preempt a destroyer's physical and emotional access to you.** Abigail avoided her mercurial husband as she executed her violence-prevention plan and later when he was drunk. Thus she limited his opportunities to endanger himself or others.

8. **Allow the destroyer to absorb the consequences of malevolent, self-absorbed, and selfish behaviors.** Abigail used family valuables to deflect violence, allowing Nabal to absorb the high price of his menacing behavior. By staking her claim to the *Washington Post,* Katharine Graham also refused to protect her husband from loss of corporate power and social status resulting from his own abusive behaviors.

9. **Follow the verbal rule for destroyer deflection: Less is more!** Use few words. Establish firm limits. Abigail executed her family-rescue plan without consulting her alcohol-soaked spouse. Devalued daughter Sharon stopped contacting her parents daily, which led them

to seek her out. Recovering cocaine addict Jesse gently set limits for his mother but avoided debates over his decisions. Decisive, resolute souls often find their challenges more successful and less conflictual when they combine few words with clear action.

If you see your family patterns here, it's time. *Now.* Make your plan. Execute it carefully and diplomatically but decisively. Rejecting the life-crippling tactics of your family, avoid any sense of arrogance, retaliation, coldness, or hostility; assume a position of moral strength as you stake claim to healthy roles and relationships.

Your life is far too precious to be wasted and desecrated by family tyrants.

PLAN FOR TRANSFORMATION

- **Begin working toward freedom by strengthening your internal radar**
- **Draw upon positive aspects of your personality and character**
- **Determine what price you are willing to pay for freedom**
- **Set firm boundaries for healthy roles and relationships**

TRANSFORMING HABIT
Seek one-on-one relationships with each member
of your family.

SEVEN

REACH FOR CONNECTION

The air was thick with tension as two generations of bitterness and rage met in my office.

To my right was the wayward patriarch, Wade. His wife, Lana, had locked Wade into celibate Siberia. She reminded him daily of the violence done to her heart by his two-year affair. Even though the details of the affair had been revealed three years before, Lana still used Wade's guilt as a bludgeon to even the score.

Wade and Lana's grown children, Rita and Skip, had entered the office first, claiming the love-seat sofa to my left, preventing their parents from having to sit together. Lana nudged her chair closer to the sofa while Wade sank deeper into the wingback chair several feet away.

Without a word, logistics told the story. Dad was the outsider disdained by all. For three years, Rita and Skip had refused to visit their parents' home when their dad was present, except briefly on holidays. Both parents had become toxic to their children, who were weary of the tension generated at the top of the family system.

TAKING A RISK FOR CONNECTION

Intensely grieved by his own failures, by the contempt seeping from Lana, and by estrangement from his disillusioned adult children, Wade was desperate for relief that could not come from popping a couple of Excedrin.

> COUPLES WHO IDENTIFIED AND CORRECTED THEIR OWN DYSFUNCTIONAL ROLES IN THEIR FAMILY OF ORIGIN MADE GREATER PROGRESS IN MARITAL RELATIONS THAN COUPLES FOCUSED EXCLUSIVELY ON MARITAL COUNSELING.

To help this family find the comfort it craved, I decided to use strategies shaped by Georgetown University's Murray Bowen, who preferred to send clients back to the scene of the crime for resolution. Bowen sent clients home to deal directly with the family of origin, to pry themselves out of the family emotional system, to detach from family triangles, and to assume roles that encourage maturation throughout the family.

In the process, Bowen was startled by this discovery: Couples who identified and corrected their own dysfunctional roles in their family of origin made greater progress in marital relations than couples focused exclusively on marital counseling. By dealing with issues each partner brought into the relationship, the spouses' natures were transformed, triggering metamorphosis in the marriage.

But I also drew on the work of clinical pioneer James Framo, who promoted multigenerational clinical sessions to make more rapid progress than may be possible through individual counseling.[1]

Wade's family was about to test Framo's strategy.

Primed to unleash bottled-up bitterness in our initial two-hour session, Wade's family was startled by my first inquiry.

"Later, we will explore family wounds," I told them. "First, I'd like you to look around this room and answer this question: What is one positive quality or happy memory that you attach to each person?" I asked them to speak directly to that person, not to me. As they spoke, I recorded statements on giant sheets of paper.

Tension mounted. *A positive quality in betrayer Wade? A happy memory about Wade?* I was met with grim faces and silence.

I was not siding with Wade, nor did I have any intention of shielding him from accountability. The stark reality was that this patriarch now functioned from a position sabotaged by his own choices. But he was, in his weakened state, making a risky bid for connection. For that, he deserved enormous credit.

EXCAVATED TRUTH

I was strategically moving this family toward truth telling. Partial truth can prove as diabolical as lies, elevating victims to near sainthood and demonizing villains who inevitably are not the only ones ravaging the family.

As they mined their past for positive memories, family members could begin to move away from their natural tendency to inflate personal goodness and exaggerate the malevolence of others. "Who will be first?" I asked the family seated before me.

Skip volunteered, starting with his mother. "You were always there for me, Mom. You must have thrown me a thousand baseballs in the backyard, and you even helped me buy junky ol' Jimmy." They both laughed at memories of bright green Jimmy—Skip's five-hundred-dollar first car.

"Rita, no matter how much I tormented you, I was amazed at how you kept such a cool head," added Skip, "except maybe when I spied on your dates!" As the family chuckled at teenage offenses now muted with time, the atmosphere brightened a bit more.

Finally, Skip turned to his dad, silent at first. Tension thickened as words emerged slowly from a passive face. "Dad," he choked out, "you took me fishing and camping a few times, and I wanted even more."

I wanted even more . . .

You weren't there enough was Skip's covert hit. But he was also delivering a treasure for his dad's heart, if only Wade could detect and savor it: *I needed and wanted you, Dad!*

Skip was bridging a huge gap. If the family acknowledged that this father was once valued, if they reconnected emotionally with the desirable Wade, there was hope that his genuine remorse could be accepted.

Rita, Lana, and finally Wade took turns facing each family member to directly affirm positive qualities and memories.

For the first time in years, they all engaged in wholesome eyeball-to-eyeball communication. No more using Mom as a middleman to communicate with Dad. No more verbal bombs. These factors alone reduced emotional static, helping each person stay in his or her own skin without getting sucked into the game of defending or representing another party.

The climate continued to shift, particularly when comments were made to Wade.

"I probably would have flunked out if you hadn't spent hours helping me with algebra," noted Rita. Despite her anger, she was admitting, *You did make a positive difference in my life, Dad.*

"You always provided well for the family. No matter what was going on," admitted Lana, "I never had to chase you down for money."

No matter what was going on . . .

Lana gave Wade credit: He *did* run around with a mistress and later separated from his wife, but he did *not* risk the family's financial security. Lana knew too many women who, unlike herself, were not only dumped but left destitute by a deserting spouse. She was grateful to escape their fate.

Prior to this moment, Lana's unspoken loyalty test for her children required a scorched-earth policy against Wade: *Burn his image, burn his reputation, burn anything positive that he ever did. Otherwise, you betray Mom.* Lana's dominant voice previously suppressed any divergent views. But now this matriarch revised her own loyalty test: *The world will not implode if we acknowledge specks of goodness in this man.*

Wade needed this boost of positive encouragement in order

to endure the emotional onslaught that came in the next phase of this process.

EQUALIZING THE BLAME GAME

Plastering a huge sticky sheet of positive qualities and memories to the wall, I cleared the way for *negative* family perspectives of Wade, Lana, Rita, and Skip. "Each of you will now hear statements that may feel threatening, so prepare your mind," I warned. All four would describe one negative trait or distasteful memory about each other person in the room. "Try not to be defensive but to listen for truth. Ask yourself: *Is the statement valid? What am I willing to do about it?*"

We were about to integrate negative truth with positive truth in order to clarify realities about each family member. Some would be hit harder than others. Obviously, the initial hostility was laser-fixed on Wade, but each family member was in for surprises, starting with Rita.

On his round of the room, brother Skip remarked, "Rita, you've always been bossy. Even now. Holidays have to be *your* way. Events with Mom, *your* way. You're the big sister, but I'm twenty-six with my own family, so you and I need to have a more balanced adult relationship."

Rita's eyes grew big and focused on her brother. She asked for more specifics about the role he'd like in the family and appeared to soak in his message.

Turning to his mother, Skip's voice was gentle. "Mom, you've relied on me as the man in your life. But my plate is full with my own wife and kids. You've actually become more capable over the years and can do more for yourself.

And Dad is more available now to do lots of the stuff you ask from me. So I'd like you to lean on me only when you really *need* to," concluded Skip, "not just every time you *want* to."

The room was silent. Lana long ago transferred dependence from her husband to her children, using them as surrogate spouses. They grew weary of this routine but pitied her too much to complain. Seeing herself as a perpetual victim, Lana expected others to protect her from criticism or demands.

As truth was pried out of this family, more complex images of demoralizing, controlling, and codependent behaviors emerged. The entire family colluded in a dance of alienation and pain.

Skip's harshest words were directed at Wade. "Dad, the truth is you left me without a father many years before the mistress came along. Never once did you make it to a championship game. Basketball. Tennis. Football. You name it. All the other guys had dads there, but not *my* dad," said Skip. "Then, after a while, it wasn't just your job. It was that woman. Funny how you could make time for her but not for us. You threw us away like trash."

So his family's rage was not all about the mistress, as Wade believed. Feelings of distance and rejection convulsed this family long before Wade's affair.

Skip was controlled as he spoke. His words were not soaked in venom or hurled as verbal bombs. Red eyes punctuated the pain as he talked. His message seemed valid, not exaggerated.

The room was silent. Wade's own eyes were red as he

absorbed his son's anguish. He quietly listened as his daughter and wife took their turn.

The process came full circle, back to Wade as grief-speaker. He was not in the mood to critique anyone in this room. But we were there to establish honest relationships between authentic personalities, so Wade had to speak as well.

To his daughter and son, the message was the same. "You say you want a father, that you want a relationship. But you are so full of rage, I am locked out. Totally. I don't want off the hook. But if you refuse even to talk to me, how can I know what to do? I'd like to have dinner with each of you soon to explore one-on-one what you want from me."

At last Wade turned to his wife. "Lana, I spent years begging you to go with me on trips. I invited you to dinner with my friends. There were always reasons you couldn't: the kids, church, an art class," Wade said, his voice trembling. "I take full responsibility for choices that ripped into your heart. I'm not shifting blame. I'm just trying to say I wanted to be closer. But the answer always seemed to be 'No!'"

"I can't deny this," said Lana quietly, "and I'm sorry."

"I want very much to try again," added Wade.

"This will be very hard," replied Lana. "I'm terrified that I will be hurt by you."

This was a new Lana—speaking her fear, not her rage. Her words had a visible effect on Wade. His face softened. Fear was much more approachable than fury.

Within hours, a seismic shift had occurred in this family, as villains and victims alike were demystified.

Fitting his villain image, Wade had gouged huge holes in the hearts of his wife and children. He admitted this, expressed great remorse, and desperately asked them to help him find ways to atone.

There is another, equally valid side to Wade. In rare self-reflection, he spoke of the frightening death of his mother, then the loss of his father to widower's grief and to work. From the age of ten, Wade was emotionally abandoned and on his own. So he unwittingly did the same to his children: he orphaned them while he was still alive. Or so it seemed.

Wade had hoped for a warm, loving relationship with his wife and children as a refuge for his heart. He tried but failed. Lana, in return, rebuffed him, turning to her children for intimacy.

Tied tight to a mother who excluded their father, the children imitated Lana. They rejected Wade's attempts to connect but blamed him for the distance. When he yielded to their attempts to push him to the periphery of family life, they resented him for desertion. For years he lived in an emotional desert chosen by Lana, not himself. When his longings for warmth and human connection led to forbidden love, he became the full-blown family villain.

As for Lana, she had learned early to distance herself from a blaming, rejecting father. She and her childlike mother clung to each other for support, and Lana pursued warm, supportive relations outside the family to compensate for the coldness within. Minor disagreements with Wade early in marriage triggered the survival strategy programmed deeply within Lana:

- Distance myself from this wounding man
- Build solidarity with others in the family as a united front against pain from him
- Substitute outsiders for the detached father/husband

Like pieces of a life-sized jigsaw puzzle coming together, each new bit of Wade and Lana's history produced a fuller picture of their lives. They had responded to each other as they had been programmed to do by early relationships. Wade's passivity, which he used to protect himself from futile hopes for affection as a child, now sabotaged his marriage. His withdrawal perpetuated Lana's own habit of rejection, and her disdain reinforced his flight from pain.

REPAIR EFFORTS CAN RESCUE A RELATIONSHIP FROM GROWING CONFLICT AND HELP RESTORE WARMTH.

Both Wade and Lana had failed at repair attempts that, note relationship experts John Gottman and Nan Silver, prevent "negativity from escalating out of control."[2] Injections of humor into stressed conversations, expressions of agreement or sympathy during disputes, admission of guilt, or timely apologies are repair efforts that can rescue a relationship from growing conflict and help restore warmth.

As truth gradually clarified the distorted mental images this family held of each other, compassion, empathy, and remorse grew, not only in the parents' hearts, but within the hearts of their adult children as well.

EMOTIONAL EXITS

Wade, Lana, Rita, and Skip were impulsively reactive to each other, a family pattern that "exaggerates and calcifies differences," explains Harriet Lerner in *The Dance of Intimacy*.[3] As conflict grows and opposition becomes more rigid, family members are sucked into emotional intensity.

What can you do when this pattern erupts in your family? If you dare to pull out of your family's emotional field through the following steps, you're likely to see calmer, more positive interactions between family members.[4]

- **Tone down the reactivity,** expressed through over-reaction to others' beliefs, speech, or behaviors, which distracts focus from the one person you can improve: *yourself*.

- **Shift focus from others** in a family's high-voltage emotional field to clarify and correct your own feelings, roles, and responsibilities—regardless of choices others make.

- **Pursue one-on-one connections:** Speak and respond directly to each parent and sibling, taking responsibility for your own communication, perceptions, and responses.

- **Deactivate middlemen,** who tend to worsen gossip, misunderstanding, conflict, and barriers in families that can be much calmer and closer when individuals work out differences directly with each other.

- **Seek a calm inner core** when confronted with deep family emotion, a skill demonstrated by Wade. His remarkable calmness when besieged during family sessions gave the others the freedom to vent buried rage, be heard, work it out, and move on.

TRIANGULATION TREACHERY

As Rita and Skip began to engage in direct dialogue with their father, they were able to break out of a dangerous triangle, with the two-child bloc serving as one corner linking two parent corners. In the past, their mother had aligned herself with the children against Wade. By responding coldly to Wade in front of their children from the time they were young, she sent emotionally blackmailing messages that told them affection to Dad was betrayal of her. Rita and Skip had long ago concluded that a relationship with their father was not worth the cost of losing the relationship with their mom.

Unconsciously, Lana and her children had developed a pincher strategy to pressure Wade. But such two-against-one formations sabotage an environment for healing. The children only served to reinforce Lana's negative reactivity. When shunned by both his children and his wife, Wade spiraled into ever deeper confusion, anger, and hopelessness—"justifying" even more contempt from his estranged family.

Deactivate the triangle

Rita and Skip had avoided their dad partly out of their own hurt, but more to evade Lana's retaliatory wrath. During the family sessions, Wade invited Rita and Skip on separate business trips to New York and California, with extended time for sightseeing and long talks. Both accepted this offer of one-on-one uncensored time with their father—the first such opportunity in years.

Each child also planned time to spend alone with Lana to cultivate healthier individual relationships with her. We set up new ground rules for these visits with each parent and between siblings:

OFFENDERS SHOULD BE GIVEN AN OPPORTUNITY TO UNDERSTAND AND CORRECT OFFENSES WITHOUT THE MINDS OF OTHER FAMILY MEMBERS BEING POISONED AGAINST THEM.

- **No griping or gossip about other family members.** If one was annoyed at another, the policy was to complain directly to the offender or not at all. If griping started, the listener had the right and responsibility to stop the discussion, declining to listen or respond. Offenders were to be given an opportunity to understand and correct offenses without the minds of other family members being poisoned against them.
- **Each family member was to speak for himself or herself only.** No solitary voice would speak for all, as if loyalty required a cloned brain.

Perhaps no one executes such strategies perfectly. But relationships require patience, courage, and nurture—not perfection—for healing to occur.

Cultivate forgiveness

Remembering the details of past traumas and mourning our losses are important for healing. In doing so, we can actually readjust the emotional functions of our brains. By processing the grief, we can reduce our obsession with dark memories and better control the impact of painful life events.[5]

Through concentrated family encounters, Wade, Lana, Rita, and Skip offered each other exactly such opportunity. They chose to endure dark emotions in one another—anger,

---

FORGIVENESS FORMULA

- Admission of guilt, as when Wade confessed his affair and Lana acknowledged her own rejecting behaviors.

- Repentance and apology, as when Wade expressed sorrow for violence done to Lana's heart. Lana also offered regret for long-term rejection of Wade. Confession, repentance, and apology by the offender make the forgiver's job easier.

- Painful emotions accepted by the family as part of the healing process.

- Detailed descriptions of wounds felt by victims, helping them feel heard and giving the offender greater understanding of the pain he or she inflicted.

- Historic exploration of both offender's and victim's life, which does not justify wrong but does expose ways in which wounds flow from people who themselves are wounded.

- Revision of the family story, demythologizing villains and victims alike through more complete facts and histories.

- Fairer distribution of fault, responsibility, and compassion through fuller truth.

- Empathy for the walking wounded regardless of the victim, villain, scapegoat, or hero roles played out in the family.

---

sorrow, blame, anxiety—exploring details of shared pain. Eventually, the time they spent together resulted in fewer distressing reactions. Their venture included many of the research-proven forgiveness predictors in the chart on the previous page.

Experts debate an additional point to the forgiveness formula. Some believe victims must make a deliberate decision to forgive. Others insist that forgiveness follows rather than precedes inner healing, as the victim's identity becomes less entwined with emotional injuries. This view sees forgiveness as an evolving emotional, spiritual, and cognitive process rather than a moment-in-time act of the will.[6]

Consider the following two aspects of forgiveness:

- **Emotional forgiveness** progresses as a victim's negative feelings of bitterness, resentment, and hatred evolve into empathy, sympathy, compassion, and even care for the offender.
- **Behavioral forgiveness** flows out of internal decisions and feelings. Even victims who still ache with a sense of betrayal or wounding can choose acts of mercy and grace, offering pardon where there is injury and love where there is hatred. They may also choose not to shun or avoid their offender nor seek revenge. Sometimes such relationship-soothing behaviors encourage emotional healing for both parties, but for others such repair attempts come only after the victim has gained some relief from emotional injury.

What about unrepentant family offenders who habitually leave severely violated and wounded victims in their wake?

Even the Bible can be confusing on this issue. Jesus declared: "If someone strikes you on the right cheek, turn to him the other also. . . . I tell you: Love your enemies and pray for those who persecute you" (Matthew 5:39, 44).

But what was Jesus' response:

- to the disciples who fell asleep on the job when he was facing death (Matthew 26:36-41)?
- to the hypocritical Pharisees scheming to trap him in a political and theological ambush (Matthew 22:18-22)?
- to crooked money changers cheating the poor (Matthew 21:12-13)?

While the Bible commands forgiveness, mercy, and grace, it likewise calls for moral accountability and courageous confrontation of evil.

Jesus confronted moral laziness within his surrogate family—the disciples. He exposed the conniving, malicious nature of the Pharisees on their terms—in public, where they sought to turn private resentment into public spectacle and entrap him. And he physically blocked more swindling of poor worshippers at the Temple.

WHILE THE BIBLE COMMANDS FORGIVENESS, MERCY, AND GRACE, IT LIKEWISE CALLS FOR MORAL ACCOUNTABILITY AND COURAGEOUS CONFRONTATION OF EVIL.

Forgiveness that minimizes

the moral or material debt owed by the offender can invite more violations of self and others. Forced forgiveness can also cause more grief for the victim and villain alike.

RISKY FORGIVERS AND GRUDGE ADDICTS

Sometimes forgiveness can actually stand in the way of remorse and squelch repentance from the person who has offended you. Take a look at the following examples of risky forgiver responses, as expressed by Case Western Reserve University researchers:

- "That's okay" (condoning, denying that a debt exists)
- "It's no big deal" (minimizing the debt that is owed)
- "I know you've been under a lot of stress lately" (justifying the violator's behavior)[7]

Such feeble responses convolute concepts of mercy, grace, and justice and instead reinforce a culture that rejects moral absolutes, accountability, and responsibility.

At the opposite victim extreme are grudge addicts who reject all mercy and grace in order to sustain an edge over their moral debtors. Gottman and Silver warn that hope for healing is bleak if you choose one of these four responses rather than forgiveness: criticism, contempt, defensiveness, or stonewalling.[8]

Grudge addicts contaminate the lives they touch with hostility, heartache, and hopelessness. Their contagious anger and resentment exact enormous costs.

Venom-filled families are a prescription not only for agony

but for debilitating disease and even death. Researchers have found that when husbands and wives hold grudges and reject reconciliation, the resulting stress fuels a 35 percent higher illness rate and shortens one's life span by an average of four years.[9]

A DE-STRESSED MIND LEADS TO STUNNING HEALTH IMPROVEMENT. EVEN MORE DRAMATIC ARE THE RESULTS OF LOVE INJECTIONS INTO A DISEASEWRACKED BODY.

Sixty to 90 percent of all doctor visits in the United States can be traced to stress, which sabotages the cardiovascular, digestive, and immune systems, often with lethal effects. In contrast, a de-stressed mind leads to stunning health improvement.[10] Even more dramatic are the results of love injections into disease-wracked bodies. In *Spontaneous Healing*, Andrew Weil, MD, describes patients whose symptoms of severe autoimmune diseases—including rheumatoid arthritis and lupus, as well as musculoskeletal pain and chronic fatigue—disappeared when the patient fell in love.[11]

As it turns out, Solomon nailed both scientific and spiritual truth when he declared, "A cheerful heart is good medicine, but a crushed spirit dries up the bones" (Proverbs 17:22).

But as Virginia Commonwealth University psychology professor Everett Worthington says, reconciliation is not one-sided but is "earned through mutually trustworthy behavior on the part of both people."[12]

Sometimes reconciliation is elusive. What then? The first step toward personal heart repair is to embrace an objective view of the current relationship and its history. Seek to gain understanding, empathy, and compassion both for yourself and those who have offended you. And, finally, nurture your faith, for "faith quiets the mind like no other form of belief, short-circuiting the nonproductive reasoning that so often consumes our thoughts," advises Harvard's Herbert Benson in *Timeless Healing*.[13]

As marriages tend to settle into volatile, avoidant, or validating patterns, say John Gottman and Joan DeClaire in *The Relationship Cure,* so do families. A family can make a quantum shift from volatile or avoidant to validating if just one solitary soul chooses a peacemaking strategy.

A family-peacemaker strategy can produce remarkable healing in relationships. But some determined family peacemakers discover that no effort seems to work. After heroic efforts to repair relationships, they are confronted with more emotional blackmail, rejection, and even hatred in the family. When this occurs, surrogate family connections are worth a closer look. Imported lovers of your heart not only can be powerful healing agents but can literally transform personal destiny.

FAMILY-PEACEMAKER STRATEGY

- Exit the high-voltage family emotional field
- Detriangulate
- Provide a calm presence
- Downgrade reactivity
- Offer affirmation
- Seek one-on-one connections

FIND YOUR HEART-WARMERS

In the case of one young son of a blueblood British family, a surrogate mother, Elizabeth Anne Everest—aka "Woom"— seemed not only to transform destiny for *him,* but quite likely for the rest of us as well.

Hired to care for the infant son of Lord Randolph Churchill, Woom filled a huge void in Winston's heart. At the time, nannies in upper-class England typically delivered children for parental visits by appointment. Randolph and Jennie Churchill eliminated even that routine, abdicating nearly all their parenting responsibilities to servants and relatives.

Jennie, a stunning American beauty, was derailed from maternal duty by a series of powerful lovers, including England's King Edward. Randolph, a spectacular political star and member of Parliament, needed no distractions. He seemed truly repulsed by Winston, refusing to see him for long periods. When forced to spend time with the child, he assaulted him with scathing verbal attacks.

When Winston was seven, his mother took him to the train station and sent him off alone for his first trip to boarding school. He arrived in darkness, quite terrified. He should have been, as he was soon savagely attacked and sent fleeing into the woods by school bullies. The sadistic headmaster also beat the boys severely, as Woom discovered on one of Winston's trips home when she found his back and bottom covered by wounds.

For two years, the Churchills ignored Winston's plight until Woom finally convinced Jennie to examine her son's back. Transferred to another school, Winston was left aching and desperate for signs of affection from his mother and father.

COME HOME TO WHOSE HEART?

Woom was "my dearest and most intimate friend," Winston wrote many years later.[14] When his parents inevitably left him alone for Christmas and other holidays, Woom took him to celebrate with her brother's family in their simple cottage. An assistant prison warden, Woom's brother read great literature to Winston at night. Through Woom, Winston gained character-molding infusions of care not only from a deeply dedicated surrogate mother but also from an entire surrogate family.

For all this, Woom truly became a chief love in Winston's life, and he kept her picture in his bedroom until he died. For Woom's faithful service, the nanny and family servant was dismissed after nineteen years, penniless, surviving only through the care of her sisters and Winston himself.

WINSTON CHURCHILL GAINED CHARACTER-MOLDING INFUSIONS OF CARE — FROM AN ENTIRE SURROGATE FAMILY.

As Woom was dying, her family sent for her cherished Winston, who held the hand of his beloved nanny as she breathed her last. Now a young officer in Her Majesty's army, Winston paid for Woom's headstone and inscribed his name beneath hers.

As we saw earlier, boys molded by their parents' rejection, coldness, and physical and verbal abuse often are social time bombs. Winston got a massive dose of rejection and physical abuse during his early years. Some soul-deadening families produce multiple children crippled by isolation, addiction, incarceration, homelessness, and despondency—except those children who receive special attention from a teacher, neighbor, friend, or other outsiders.

SURPRISING SURROGATES

For Winston, the antidote for debilitating despair was more than just Woom and her family. Strange as it may seem, his mother's well-connected lovers often took pity on the father-hungry Winston, and he eagerly drank in their attention, as detailed in *The Last Lion: Winston Spencer Churchill* by William Manchester.[15]

One such Jennie suitor, U.S. congressman Bourke Cockran, squired Winston around New York City and introduced the young Brit to President William McKinley, New York governor Theodore Roosevelt, and a slew of judges.

The congressman also gave Winston his first sampling of Edmund Burke's works, treating his young guest as a peer. After cold rejection by his own father, Winston was so inspired by Cockran's careful attention that he wrote of him in glowing terms nearly forty years later.

Cockran could not have guessed that he was investing in a future British prime minister and perhaps the most pivotal politician of the twentieth century. Without a politically inspired Winston Churchill, surely the destinies of Europe and America could have taken a drastically different turn.

The brilliant Christian intellectual C. S. Lewis had an experience remarkably like Churchill's. After losing his mother to death when he was nine, he was sent by his overwhelmed father to boarding school. The school's clergyman headmaster, "Oldie," unleashed irrational and unpredictable violence on students and in time was diagnosed as psychotic, reports Harvard's Armand Nicholi Jr. in *The Question of God: C. S. Lewis and Sigmund Freud Debate God, Love, Sex, and the Meaning of Life.*[16]

Seeking to salvage his son's education, Lewis's father hired a gifted tutor, William T. Kirkpatrick. The young Lewis became deeply attached to Kirkpatrick—an atheist. Lewis jettisoned his family's Christianity and embraced atheism, prodded partly by Oldie's brutalization and partly by Kirkpatrick's kindness.

Seeing the face of one who loves is seeing the face of God. God is love, and those who love are conduits of God's nature.

DERIVED FROM 1 JOHN 4:16-21

After a dramatic conversion many years later, Lewis was catapulted to the apex of Christian intellectuals and writers. But he remained deeply fond of Kirkpatrick, who was a surrogate father to him. While Lewis proclaimed that his whole being and energy were committed to the ultimate destination of heaven, he wrote of Kirkpatrick, "My debt to him is very great, my reverence to this day undiminished."[17]

Given Lewis's matchless ability to speak to saint and skeptic alike, the rest of us are no doubt indebted to Kirkpatrick as well.

Notable here is Lewis's integrity—giving honest credit to an atheist in a manner surely confusing to many Christians who revere Lewis's work. Also notable is his heart's desperate hunger for human affection, and the human tendency to lap it up wherever it was offered.

Finally, here is a theological reality: Seeing the face of one who loves *is* seeing the face of God (1 John 4:16-21). God *is* love, and those who love are conduits of God's nature—whether they consciously embrace him or not.

MENTAL RESURRECTION OF ALL SORTS OF OLD LOVE IMAGES — NOT JUST ROMANTIC FIGURES — CAN RETROFIT A PERSON'S INNER WORLD EMOTIONALLY, PSYCHOLOGICALLY, AND SPIRITUALLY, NURTURING THE HEART AGAIN AND AGAIN.

Long after Woom gave young Winston Churchill sanctuary in her heart and long after William Kirkpatrick offered emotional and intellectual refuge to C. S. Lewis, the mere thought of these surrogates seemed to stir deep feelings of affection, gratitude, and reverence in Churchill and Lewis. Such is the awesome power of evocative memory—memories that rekindle original feelings stirred by caring personalities.

Evocative memory has helped numerous victims of depression, anxiety, panic attacks, and phobias overcome emotional suffering by deliberately shifting their focus to loving childhood figures. Mental resurrection of all sorts of old love images—not just romantic figures—can retrofit a person's inner world emotionally, psychologically, and spiritually, nurturing the heart again and again.

Those who choose positive thoughts are able to take greater control of their minds. In therapy, clients use this concept to find relief from troubling emotions. Once they've stabilized their own emotional turmoil, they have more energy to protect and nurture the relationships that are most important to them. At that point, many clients feel little or no need for ongoing therapy.

But psychologists did not invent the concept of powerful mind-mood-relationship connections. The mental-health advisory to rivet the mind to whatever is true, honest, just, pure, lovely, virtuous, and worthy of praise "and the God of peace shall be with you" (Philippians 4:8-9, KJV) originated a couple of millennia ago. Choosing to focus on those who have offered gifts of care, direction, faith, integrity, character, perseverance, optimism, or human connection opens up a gentler world than one poisoned by tormentors.

Who are your heart-warmers, especially those who gave to you when you were a child? Which old loves—relatives, neighbors, teachers, friends—insulated your heart with care, encouraged self-reliance and independence, and squelched self-pity? Who offered hope in your despair? Who would you link with the qualities listed in the chart

> THE MENTAL-HEALTH ADVISORY TO RIVET THE MIND TO WHATEVER IS TRUE, HONEST, JUST, PURE, LOVELY, VIRTUOUS, AND WORTHY OF PRAISE "AND THE GOD OF PEACE SHALL BE WITH YOU" (PHILIPPIANS 4:8-9, KJV) ORIGINATED A COUPLE OF MILLENNIA AGO.

below? In what ways did you absorb some of these qualities from such relationships?

As you complete and reflect upon this chart, you can gain ongoing empowerment from the heart-warmers in your life.

Heart-warmers offer armor for the ongoing battles of life. Survivor personalities, notes Harvard's Gina O'Connell Higgins, tend to recruit surrogates who lighten their load

MY HEART-WARMERS

Traits	Matching Names
Caring physically	
Generous with time and resources	
Self-reliant and industrious	
Truth lover	
Emotionally stable	
Rejects victim role	
Full of faith	
Optimistic	

from childhood on, who instill a sense of self-esteem and cultivate competence. The resilient seek noble, nurturing connections and wring maximum gain from these encounters.[18]

I know that many outside of my home will touch the minds
and hearts of my own children for good or ill. My prayer is
that God will guide them to the right mentors. I hope that my
son and daughter will be enriched, as I have been, by relationships with those who love truth, who are compassionate, who
seek goodness, who smile at the future, who are industrious
and self-reliant, and who are full of faith.

Relationships are our destiny. Good relationships are treasures of life to seek, embrace, and celebrate. And to remember
again and again.

PLAN FOR TRANSFORMATION

- Identify and admit positive traits in every family member,
  including those viewed as treacherous
- Identify and admit negative traits in every family
  member, including those viewed as saints or heroes
- Enact a do-not-react policy to negative family emotions:
  anger, resentment, spite, jealousy, self-pity
- Pursue one-on-one family relations without middlemen
- Cultivate forgiveness
- Recruit and cherish surrogate heart-warmers

TRANSFORMING HABIT
Embrace a vibrant connection with God.

EIGHT

WOW! FAITH FAMILIES

When clients arrive at my door with wrenching family problems, I sometimes send them home with world-famous pediatric neurosurgeon Ben Carson. As I do not know the renowned Johns Hopkins medical marvel personally, my clients must make do with a dose of Carson via video and books.

By age thirty-three, Dr. Carson was named Johns Hopkins' director of pediatric neurosurgery. He now performs some four hundred surgeries each year, often carving deep into cranial territory. I don't ask this medical genius for brain surgery on my clients. I do, however, hope that a sort of mind transplant will occur as they discover in him thought and behavior habits that can liberate their families from failure, conflict, and misery.

Ben Carson, an African-American, was born to a mother who believes she was one of perhaps twenty-four children. She only knows part of her family because she spent most of her childhood being bounced around among foster homes. At thirteen, she was whisked away by a charming minister, and years after their marriage, she bore two sons, Curtis and Ben. When the minister was exposed as a bootlegger and bigamist, the family ripped apart, leaving Sonja a poor single mom.

As Sonja Carson worked fifteen-hour days to support her sons, her boys floundered in school. Ben was rated by himself and peers as the dumbest in his class. With a third-grade education, Sonja couldn't read and was desperate to rescue her boys from her own destitute life.

Praying for wisdom, she began to implement a specific parenting strategy. In addition to regular church activities for her boys, she restricted them to very limited TV viewing, and only after all schoolwork was completed. She also required them to write two book reports every week. They reluctantly but diligently complied with their mother's demands, unaware that she couldn't actually read their reports.

Within months, Ben's reading regimen catapulted him from class dummy to class star, dwarfing all academic competition. But his troubled history had brewed deep rage within him. During one out-of-control conflict he lunged for his teenage friend with a knife and was blocked only by a belt buckle. Realizing instantly how close he'd come to landing his brilliant mind in jail, he retreated to his bathroom, where for hours he sat on the edge of the tub reading Proverbs and begging God for inner control.

Carson emerged from that bathroom, he says, transformed. This newfound emotional stability meshed with a stellar scientific mind that then powered him into Yale, where he met a music major who captured his heart. Married in 1975, Ben and Candy Carson attend church together regularly and still "hold hands like young lovers," reports the *Washington Post* in a three-page August 2002 feature on this rescuer of children stalked by death.[1]

"He performs miracles," says Dan Angel, a Hollywood producer who, with Whoopi Goldberg, is planning a movie on Carson's life. This is one Hollywood movie that could transform lives if it captures the major secrets of Carson's rise from a Detroit ghetto to global medical fame.

As a teenager, Ben Carson's growing sense of positive identity, self-control, responsibility, and faith in people was predictable. Adolescents energized by faith not only show such internal advantages, but also enjoy increased patterns of academic success and peer leadership. While faith is shown as a driving force behind youth achievement, it is also proven as a powerful protector against teen drug and alcohol abuse, premarital sex, promiscuity, delinquency, and criminality.

WHILE FAITH IS SHOWN AS A DRIVING FORCE BEHIND YOUTH ACHIEVEMENT, IT IS ALSO PROVEN AS A POWERFUL PROTECTOR AGAINST TEEN DRUG AND ALCOHOL ABUSE, PREMARITAL SEX, PROMISCUITY, DELINQUENCY, AND CRIMINALITY.

But faith is no magic bullet guaranteeing a pain-free life, as discovered by the Virginia family of a dynamic Christian teenager named Emily. This family's journey differed dramatically from that of the Carsons, offering crucial lessons in healing for the rest of us.

WALK-ON-WATER STRATEGY

As John settled into the wingback chair and Dale Patricia snuggled into the love seat in my office, the grim expressions on their faces reflected an inner pain that can come only from great loss. Their teenage daughter, Emily, had died unexpectedly eighteen months prior to our visit.

Silence filled the room. First Dale's eyes turned red, then John's. Softly, I spoke. "Let's talk about Emily."

Emily's story tumbled out. As a junior at the giant public high school in town, Emily had thrived as a member of the swim team. She also had loved to make music with the school's symphonic band.

Dale smiled as she recalled how on the family's last beach vacation, the spirited Emily sang Dixie Chicks hits over and over. She had several favorite sayings that she used to navigate life with parents. One was "It's U.C.," meaning "under control." If John asked, "How's your room looking?" Emily would respond, "It's U.C., Dad." Another favorite quip was "the Deal," as when she missed the school bus and John was drafted as chauffeur. Emily declared that this was part of "the Deal," his parental responsibility for her. Father and daughter often debated what was and was not part of "the Deal," with John asking, "By the way, when did I ever sign up for this deal?"

During the summer of 2000, Emily had participated in a church missions trip with the theme *WoW—Walk on Water*. Kids were challenged with the notion that to walk on water they must first, like the apostle Peter, get out of the boat and let go of the secure niches of life. Second, they must always keep their eyes on Jesus.

Emily returned from the trip inspired, but by September she seemed sluggish. Her parents knew something wasn't quite right.

First she was examined by her pediatrician, who prescribed medication. But a few days later, Emily still was not better, and after a trip to the emergency room, she was admitted to the hospital for four days of tests and exploratory surgery. Doctors made an ominous discovery during the surgery and warned Emily's parents that they must prepare for a difficult challenge.

> TO WALK ON WATER WE MUST FIRST, LIKE THE APOSTLE PETER, GET OUT OF THE BOAT AND LET GO OF THE SECURE NICHES OF LIFE.

Seventeen-year-old Emily was diagnosed with signet-ring cell adenocarcinoma of the stomach. Typically, only elderly people develop this inoperable, incurable, and very aggressive cancer. Four pathologists confirmed that Emily's body had been invaded by a rare and frightening killer. The prognosis? At best, a few months.

As Emily's father later recalled, things were not "U.C.," and this was not part of "the Deal."

Dale remembered how Brenda, a family friend, held Emily's hand as she briefly considered her dilemma. Looking at parents, friends, and medical experts gathered around her, Emily responded to the news in typical Emily fashion: "Whatever happens, it'll be okay."

John and Dale took Emily home for an extraordinary journey. "She only cried twice," said John. "Once when she said she had wanted to attend a Christian college and then have a ministry, but now that would never happen."

To the contrary, through cyberspace Emily's impact had rapidly gone global. International responses to her remarkable courage and faith were flowing like a cyberriver back to her home.

Gently easing her daughter's troubled mind, Dale said, "Look what's happening! We're getting e-mails from all over the world from people moved by your story! You are having that ministry now!"

The second time Emily cried, she said she was worried about her parents.

What wise insight from a young girl. The pain and grief Emily saw in her parents had indeed torn at their marriage.

Striving to make Emily's last weeks as comfortable as possible, hospice workers guided Dale in Emily's home care. Brenda, the same friend who sat with Emily in the hospital, came to help with her care at home. "We clung to each other with broken, yet questioning hearts," Brenda remembered.

Through nutrition pumps, fluid infusions, hot packs, and torturous pain, Emily continued to show amazing grace. Reflecting on her young life, she told her dad that her favorite memory was of leading a boy to faith in Christ.

When the pain was especially difficult, Emily asked her mother or friends to read Scripture aloud. Other times, she joined in with the family surrounding her bed, singing hymn after hymn. One afternoon, Emily shared with Brenda how much she had enjoyed a foot massage from her dad. "I love a nice foot massage, too," Brenda told her friend. Racked with cancer, Emily pledged to give her faithful friend a foot massage, a vow that made them both laugh.

Later that week, John reported that Emily was having a very painful night, so nurse Brenda rushed over to offer relief. In time, as the pain medication began to work its wonders, Emily rose from her bed, dragging pumps around the house and collecting a variety of items.

"Next thing I knew, she was in front of me with a basin of warm water and a towel draped over her shoulder. I made a move to protest and she firmly reminded me of her promise," recalled Brenda. "I sat back. She proceeded to remove my shoes and socks and wash my feet. She dried them gently and massaged them with a wonderful-smelling lavender lotion. It was a silent and sacred moment. I leaned over toward Emily's bowed head and whispered that I loved her. She replied simply, 'I know.'

"My mind envisions Jesus, the ultimate servant, who humbly washed his disciples' feet. We talked together about how Jesus' friend Mary used expensive perfume to wash his feet. I felt similarly to Emily as Jesus to Mary when he said in Matthew 26:10, 'She has done a beautiful thing to me.'"

Five weeks after the world seemed to stand still during the doctor's report, Dale held in her arms a precious daughter whose ragged breathing signaled that soon a different stillness would come. "We heard a mother's precious words to her daughter," reported Brenda. "She told Emily in a voice choking back the sobs that it was okay for her to let go, it was okay to go meet Jesus, that her mom loved her so much, that she was so special, and promised she'd see her again in the new heaven—that place where there will be no more crying and no more pain."

Sorting through her possessions later, John and Dale were stunned to discover a hymn Emily had written in June, just five months before her death and three months before the illness was exposed. Emily's spiritual focus seemed extraordinary and her parents found this apparently happy anticipation of a journey to God comforting and remarkable:

Oh, Jesus
You are so beautiful
It makes my soul cry
For the day You can hold my hand
And walk me by

The fountains of the living water
The warm golden streets that never end
Surrounded by the heavens made by the Father
This is the day when my spirit will mend

I am flying through space
Stars whizzing by
Nearing you
We will dance on the streets that are golden (emphasis added)

The Woodson High School auditorium filled with students and church friends for a joyful memorial service led by Emily's former pastor and close family friend, Charles. "Emily had cancer of the body, but not of the soul," the pastor told a hushed audience.

Emily had indeed walked on water. She had plunged out of the boat of security, keeping her eyes on Jesus. She showed us all exactly what to do if we don't want to sink. Listening to this story while maintaining a calm demeanor required all the strength I could muster. While I was the counselor sought for assistance in heart healing, it was the clients who had overwhelmed me with their story.

I felt I was on sacred ground, exploring with these parents the mix of joy and pain in remembering Emily and her impact on their lives. Joy came from her strength, faith, dignity, courage, and love for others, even as she was dying. Pain came from the enormous loss of this precious life in their family.

We want security. We want comfort. We want affluence. None of these give us freedom. But there is no such thing as certain security. . . . That is not what Jesus offered. He offered life, and life more abundantly, and that means everything, the whole spectrum, laughter and tears, joy and disappointment. . . . That is how Jesus lived, and how we are to live.

MADELEINE L'ENGLE, *BRIGHT EVENING STAR*

On July 4, 2002, just after hearing this story, I found myself at some friends' river house. This was Emily's birthday, and pausing by the river I prayed in her memory. I celebrated parents whose love for God had created for Emily an environment that encouraged her faith in God. I thanked God that such faith empowered this remarkable young woman to confront the ultimate challenge with courage, grace, and purpose. And I celebrated that, in turn, Emily's faith assured her parents a well of strength, joy, and inspiration from which they could draw forever.

Memories of Emily do not flood this family with sensations of fear, anxiety, or hopelessness. Such feelings are trumped by a triumphant sense of ultimate destiny, security, and peace that Emily and her parents shared. All of this is a sacred mystery that defies human norms.

STRATOSPHERIC HOPE

"The real story here is not Emily but the work of God in her life," insisted her mother. Dale offered potent confirmation of a mountain of new research linking an active faith to hope, resistance to despair, and emotional vitality. Experts agree that hope in God enables such trauma victims as Emily and her family to detach emotionally from their circumstances, allowing them to feel secure and even optimistic while suffering great loss.

> A MOUNTAIN OF NEW RESEARCH LINKS AN ACTIVE FAITH TO HOPE, RESISTANCE TO DESPAIR, AND EMOTIONAL VITALITY.

"An individual whose hope is grounded in a relationship with God still hopes for things of the earth," say University of Maryland medical researchers. "But if the earthly hopes meet with disappointment the individual's eternal hope allows a healthy perspective and the individual is sustained with peace and joy."[2] Hope that depends only on earthly power turns to despair when that power fails, according to the *Journal of Psychology and Theology.*

Armed with hope that offered a powerful bond to God, Emily's body was at risk during the illness but her eternal significance was not. For Emily, the meaning of her life could not be extinguished by mere death. In fact, it could be enhanced if greater goals were achieved, such as her burning desire to light others' journey to spiritual life.

Human connection

Emily and her family were not isolated like hermits during their ordeal. Instead, they were deeply rooted in one of America's 350,000 faith communities. Their social support, wrapped in communal faith, offered powerful insulation from despair and emotional inertia.

Years ago I worked with late-stage cancer patients at a Washington, D.C., hospital. The emotional contrast between white and black patients united in a journey toward death was startling. Most white patients appeared deeply depressed, lethargic, and hopeless. In contrast, many black patients seemed bathed in an almost eerie tranquility, exuding peace.

This was perplexing. Surely race alone could not explain such contrasting responses to imminent death. My attention shifted from the patients to their environment. The walls of black patients' rooms were covered with colorful cards: *Get Well Soon! We're Praying for You. Trust in God. God Bless You.*

The walls of white patients were relatively stark.

Sometimes black patients could hardly rest for all the relatives and friends trooping in to see them. Church choirs surrounded their bed to sing favorite hymns.

The white patients' journey to death was far more solitary.

Could I trust my pale perceptions to get this right? I asked a black hospital official for her take on the emotional and psychological gap between white and black cancer patients. "It's spiritual," she replied immediately, noting that the journey by black patients not only seemed much more faith-filled, but was also buffered by far more physical, emotional, and spiritual support from families and thriving faith communities.

White patients, in contrast, seemed terrified.

WHEN STRUCK BY WIDE-RANGING CANCERS OR CARDIOVASCULAR AND RESPIRATORY DISEASE, PEOPLE OF STRONG FAITH ARE MORE LIKELY TO RECOVER, AND THEY RECOVER FASTER THAN OTHER SURVIVORS.

But not pale Emily. Her parents had nurtured her in a faith-filled family, and she had examined and tested those beliefs to make them her own. This is an important point. Researchers find that people who allow "faith" to be imposed externally, mimicking family or groups to please others, are highly vulnerable to depression. But enhanced resistance to depression is seen in those who show intrinsic faith and are motivated to love God and find meaning in life's experiences through him, rather than just conform to a social environment.

These sturdy souls *metabolize* their faith—take it in, savor it, and convert it into emotional energy, mental power, and relationship glue. Metabolized faith transforms as surely as a rich protein diet transforms a malnourished child, with nutrients and child coalescing into something new.

Emily's faith exhibited such transforming power. She

exuded confidence that she *would* whiz past stars to dance on golden streets. So anchored spiritually, she became a sort of pied piper, leading the adults and adolescents around her to a deeper faith.

As demonstrated by Emily, people of strong faith are not immune to terrifying diseases. But they do show reduced rates of wide-ranging cancers and cardiovascular and respiratory disease. When struck by such illnesses, statistically they are more likely to recover, and they recover faster than other survivors. Emotionally, they show greater resistance to depression, anxiety disorders, and suicidal thinking.[3]

Church ladies' revenge

Faith is more than a spiritual aspirin for pain, suffering, fear, and disease. Although battered by enormous grief and emotional numbing from the loss of their cherished teenager, Emily's parents have rediscovered joy in each other and are using their own heartache to soothe the pain of others. Research shows they have an advantage: Faith-inspired partners whose marriages are stressed by personality conflict or external trauma are more likely than others to recover emotional intimacy.

An active faith is the strongest predictor of marital happiness and is linked to high ratings in marital satisfaction, cohesion, affection, stability, and recovery from marital crisis. People of faith, it turns out, hold the advantage in hot monogamy ratings.[4]

While Sigmund Freud warned ominously that religion produces neurotics with repressed sexuality, researchers have repeatedly reported exactly the opposite. Studies by Stanford University, *Redbook* magazine, and more lately the University of Chicago "show that church ladies (and the men who sleep with them) are among the most sexually satisfied people on the face of the planet," reports *USA Today*'s William R. Mattox.[5]

"Call It the Revenge of the Church Ladies" was the February 11, 1999, *USA Today* pre-Valentine's headline. As *Saturday Night Live*'s Church Lady might say with her nose squiggled up, "Now, isn't *that* special!"

Church ladies (and the men who sleep with them) are among the most sexually satisfied people on the face of the planet.

WILLIAM R. MATTOX, *USA TODAY*

Mattox also says that living together before marriage, popular as a test run of a potential partner, has been exposed as a "really lousy test." As one Rutgers University study reports, couples who live together before marriage are more likely to divorce than those who do not.[6]

Thus biblical concepts of "guard your heart" and "save it for marriage" are not the prescription of a God who is a cosmic killjoy, but a formula for enhanced security and intimacy in marriage.

Even *Rolling Stone* reported a beneath-the-cultural-radar movement back to biblical romance strategies. Single young adults are so hungry for such guidance that a course on the subject offered by Seattle Pacific University has attracted five hundred students annually. According to *Rolling Stone,* the faculty had expected twenty students.[7]

We use a most unfortunate idiom when we say, of a lustful man prowling the streets, that he "wants a woman." Strictly speaking, a woman is just what he does not want. He wants a pleasure for which a woman happens to be the necessary piece of apparatus. C. S. LEWIS, *THE FOUR LOVES*

Religious charlatans and faith traps

There are traps here to avoid: One trap is false faith that is not so much a reach for God as a response to social pressure or a tool of personal ambition. Those who "use" faith as leverage to secure social acceptance, material gain, or other payoffs show high incidences of depression and other psychological disorders. In families, this should slam the brakes on the use of shame, fear, or emotional bribes in order to jam spouses or children into arbitrary spiritual molds. Such coercion sabotages the very spiritual vitality supposedly sought.[8]

A second trap is a negative view of God as a stern father or as vindictive, impersonal, or controlling—harsh perceptions of God that are common in personalities burdened by a poor self-concept.[9] In contrast, those who view God as their loving, kindly Father tend to be energized by healthy affection for themselves, as Jesus himself urged (Mark 12:31).

A third trap is lone-ranger religion, as embraced by those who get their spiritual fix electronically—through radio or television.[10] Those who favor piped-in spirituality have elevated anxiety rates. But research shows that those who seek companions for their spiritual journey—as do weekly church attendees—not only inoculate themselves against anxiety, but also show dramatically reduced rates of suicide and lung, heart, and liver disease.[11] As cited earlier, they also enjoy more satisfying social and marital relations.

What if you tried Christianity or the church—and choked?
You may find a soul mate in award-winning author Philip Yancey. "I have spent most of my life in recovery from the Church," says Yancey, whose youth was shaped by harsh, authoritarian church scenes that "had mixed in lies with truth."[12] In his book *Soul Survivor,* Yancey explores factors that "helped my faith survive the church."

Love your neighbor as yourself. MARK 12:31

Another inspiring soul survivor, C. S. Lewis, also offers potent reinforcement to those violated in the name of God. In *Surprised by Joy,* Lewis describes his journey from disillusionment to atheism and back to a faith that defied religious charlatans and other enemies of the soul. [13]

As Søren Kierkegaard put it, a "defining relationship with God" provides a launching pad for a life that is deeply gratifying in purpose, productivity, and warm human connections. That relationship comes through a spiritual adventure, a journey that is more complicated for some than for others. But for all, the journey starts with one step, then another, perhaps beginning with the steps on the next page.

PLAN FOR TRANSFORMATION

- Go to the top. Bypass middlemen and seek God directly through:
  BIBLE STUDY: Bible-study guides on many subjects from Christian bookstores can make this step much easier.
  PRAYER: Speak your thoughts and desires to God without relying on a prepackaged message.
- Pursue communal spiritual growth: Seek a vibrant faith community that challenges and inspires you personally.
- Use a positive concept of God as an anchor: Focus on God as a loving, caring Father.
- Tap into faith boosters: Let books, music, and faith-based conferences inspire you.

TRANSFORMING HABIT
Exercise judicious generosity.

NINE

MY FAMILY'S
TRANSFORMATION

In 1967, Georgetown University's Murray Bowen sent shock waves through the family counseling community when he departed from an academic speech to reveal his personal story of family transformation. Successful changes in his family came from standing on his own convictions as a matter of integrity, *not to change others.*[1]

Hearing Murray Bowen's personal account, academics and psychotherapists alike were electrified not only as they saw new ways of helping clients, but also as they gained hope for resolving deeply entrenched problems in their own families.

MY STORY

Twenty-six years after Bowen's speech, I read his report from a very odd posture. Physically, I looked like a pretzel. For weeks, I had awoken each morning with a nerve pinched by a contorted vertebra. Every effort to move or straighten my back resulted in jolting pain, and prescribed muscle relaxants failed in their duty.

I had this odd suspicion that my twisted back was somehow connected to family stress. But how?

Seeking relief, I sank into a deep tub of bubbly hot water, which had not previously untwisted my back but did feel soothing. There I sat, cooking and cogitating.

I thought of people who came for help to my dear father, a fundamentalist Baptist minister. He never seemed to have a dime to his name, partly because he gave away what little money he had. This was a multigenerational pattern: During the Depression, Dad's own father had supported two neighbor families with his dependable wages as a railroad engineer. But my dad had no money to spare.

I remembered times as a child when the doorbell would ring, and there on the porch would be an entire family, barefoot and begging. They were strangers but somehow found the house of the Baptist minister and came seeking a handout.

> SUCCESSFUL CHANGES IN [BOWEN'S] FAMILY CAME FROM STANDING ON HIS OWN CONVICTIONS AS A MATTER OF INTEGRITY, NOT TO CHANGE OTHERS.

Taking them to a modest local motel, Dad would advise the manager that he would cover a week of lodging and meals for the needy family.

The next month when our own bills came due, there was no money. Limited resources had gone to rescue strangers, leaving my mother to deal with bill collectors who inevitably called when Dad was not home. As a child I felt enormous pressure from this financial stress.

Quietly, my mother asked me not to tell Dad if I needed anything, as he would surely spend three times a reasonable amount, being generous far beyond his modest means. Neither of us understood that I was being used as a buffer in the marital relationship as a stress reliever for my mother. Nor did we recognize the role reversals taking place as the child was challenged to exercise self-control, restraint, and cautious judgment in order to fill that gap in an adult.

Four decades later, I have evidence right on my bookshelf of my dad's responsiveness and of my mother's motivation for her unfortunate and stressful role as covert finance cop. My dad bought it for me: a seven-pound, 1,300-page volume he picked up when I mentioned our lack of a good dictionary.

This gargantuan *Webster's Encyclopedic Unabridged Dictionary of the English Language* requires the user to have a PhD just to plow through hundreds of pages beyond the dictionary: the origins of words; prefixes and suffixes; abbreviations; synonyms and antonyms; popular quotations; classical mythology; foreign words and phrases; students' manual; secretaries' guide; business law for laymen; business and finance; names and their meanings; the story of America in pictures; flags of the world; U.S. presidents; and the space age. This one-volume library must have cost a fortune.

I was both chagrined and grateful to receive the gilt-edged tome from my father, whose heart was so much richer than his pocket. Sadly, the colossal book was such a bear to use that I mostly stuck with our outdated but manageable dictionary.

What did such history have to do with my pretzel spine at age forty-three? It wasn't just history. It was *current*, as the pattern continued. As my aging father bled a minuscule savings account to rescue others, Mother's anxiety over losing their tiny financial cushion was being passed to me in new ways.

Each time the cycle began again with a phone call from my distressed mother, I felt that I was expected to rescue the rescuer. Frustrated, I would replenish my parents' depleted savings account, only to have it emptied again the next time my father felt called to pry someone out of a jam. Sometimes the victim's trauma was self-inflicted. Often the rescued had more financial options than my aging rescuer dad. His help at times exceeded the need, as had my elephantine dictionary.

I realized, steaming in that hot tub, that I was a major enabler. If others made poor financial decisions, they dumped the consequences on my father so they had no incentive to act more wisely the next time. Through my mother, these consequences were then passed to me, so Dad had no reason to question his own judgment. Some of this "rescue" behavior was like giving cash to the street alcoholic who happily buys more booze. Such compassion not only fails to provide food or shelter, but actually perpetuates behavior treacherous to the very person being rescued.

Mulling over Murray Bowen's example, I realized I could not force others to make better decisions, but I could certainly decide for myself!

I determined right then and there, steaming in that tub, that my behavior would change. If I was going to help others, it would be based on my own judgment of effective acts of compassion, not on imposed strategies that I had seen fail repeatedly. I would no longer injudiciously accept rescuer roles assigned by others.

Withered externally but empowered within, I left the hot tub behind to see a shocking sight reflected in the mirror. There I was, standing ramrod straight for the first time in weeks. It was as if my spine had been relieved of a crushing burden when my mind was finally purged of the distorted idea that loyalty required conformity to family habits.

> IT WAS AS IF MY SPINE HAD BEEN RELIEVED OF A CRUSHING BURDEN WHEN MY MIND WAS FINALLY PURGED OF THE DISTORTED IDEA THAT LOYALTY REQUIRED CONFORMITY TO FAMILY HABITS.

I knew I needed to inform the key party of my changing role. That was not my father, as he was never the one who drew me into the rescue plots. No, I would need to talk to my mother, the middleman.

I drove one hundred miles to have lunch with her and plunge into a level of candor uncommon in our family. I raised the issue of previous discussions over rescues gone wrong. Surely this was very difficult for her, I observed, as pressures from others' crises repeatedly turned into financial treachery for her.

As gently as I knew how, I explained that from that point on I was pursuing a new personal policy. I told my mother that I had played a negative role in family crises by supporting decisions after the fact that conflicted with my own judgment.

I sympathized with her plight and said I was sorry that she found herself caught among numerous pressures. I said that whatever decisions other adults in the family made were their business, not mine, and that she and others had every right to exercise their own judgment, regardless of my position. I concluded by saying I would live with the consequences of my own choices but would not volunteer to absorb consequences of others' decisions.

My mother was both quiet and calm during this visit. But I knew this encounter would create enormous pressure, closing the release valve for her own anxiety when family financial habits put her at risk. However, I was convinced that this not only was the right position for me but could improve functions throughout the family.

CALM FOLLOWS THE STORM

As happened in Bowen's family and among others whom he guided through this process, family calm did follow a storm in my own situation.

Having induced new family turmoil, I knew it was my responsibility to reach out in an effort to stabilize relationships. Back at home, I called my mother a few days later. She offered gruff one-word answers to my questions. I talked to Dad. I heard quiet anger in the voice of this gentle-hearted man as well, so I assumed that Mother had described our visit.

During the next few weeks, other phone discussions were as cool as the first one. I initiated contact. My mother curtly responded.

Throughout this stage, I felt uncharacteristically calm.

Good old Murray Bowen had prepared the way by sharing wisdom not only about what to do, but also what to expect.

My next move was to send clear signals that my behavioral changes were not a form of rejection, distance, or disrespect. On a Friday, I called to invite Mother and Dad for an overnight Thanksgiving visit with me and my family—their cherished son-in-law and their only grandchildren.

Mother was noncommittal. In an upbeat manner, I asked her to discuss this with Dad over the weekend. I said I would call on Monday for their response.

"Well, Mother," I inquired on Monday, "have you had a chance to discuss Thanksgiving with Dad?"

"Oh yes!" she replied, sounding quite chipper. "We think this will work out fine!"

The visit with my parents that Thanksgiving seemed to me the best we'd ever had. They appeared unusually relaxed. They expressed feelings and opinions more openly. They actually seemed more joyful, all of which I found amazing.

Most startling were the changes in my mother. A few months after my role-changing lunch with her, my mother had a discussion with Dad that was perhaps decades overdue.

At seventy-four, my dad was in many ways vibrant, but a troublesome heart ailment was forcing him into retirement, a move that would decimate an already modest income. After fifty-three years of marriage, my mother proposed that she finally take a shot at managing their finances.

In a family wrapped around very traditional roles, money management had always been a man's job. It took both courage and resolve for Mother to suggest otherwise.

Contrary to expectations, Dad immediately agreed to this experiment. As it turned out, Mother proved to be Mrs. Goldfinger. Under her management, my parents lived better on half the income than ever before, as she squeezed maximum value out of every dollar.

"You're remarkable with money!" I exclaimed about six months later. Mother's smile brimmed not only with satisfaction but relief.

"What would have happened," I mused, "if you'd made this move fifty years ago?"

Mutely, she contemplated. "A lot would have changed," she quietly replied.

"Well, you're right about *that!*" I exclaimed. "You know, the point here isn't to resent the past, but this is what I see: God brought Dad a partner with an extraordinary gift that was precisely what he needed. But you were too afraid to raise the issue. Isn't that a shame?"

Born in 1919, my mother had been foiled by many factors. Her generation was quite locked into rigid roles, regardless of the strengths or liabilities each partner brought into marriage.

Products of deeply conservative church communities, my parents were steeped in biblical concepts of male family headship that, ironically, made little room for anyone like the female finance and business whiz of Proverbs 31.

The grandson of an alcoholic, my tenderhearted father exhibited traits common to such a legacy. Predictably for male descendants of male alcoholics, he was quite a loner and tended to stuff his feelings rather than express them openly. He seemed to escape the depressed personality tied to this breed, but his very introverted, sober nature encouraged little discussion outside of theology, which engaged his interest unlike any other subject.

For such reasons, throughout half a century of marriage my mother resisted promoting herself as chief financial officer. When retirement misery loomed smack ahead of her, a drive for survival pumped her own instincts into higher gear. She shifted into a role truer to her gifts and judgment than former roles that had been imposed by outside forces.

Mother had nearly three years to manage their finances before my father's death, an experience that surely put her in a stronger position to navigate solo at age seventy-five. Several years later, she moved into a senior apartment community and is still growing socially, emotionally, and spiritually in her eighties. I see in her a surge of independent thinking, a freer spirit, and greater ability to question old borrowed beliefs about people and life.

WHEN I PRIED MYSELF OUT OF A STRESSFUL FAMILY TRIANGLE . . . A CASCADE OF HEALTHY SHIFTS RICHOCHETED THROUGHOUT THE FAMILY.

As predicted by Murray Bowen's work, when I pried myself out of a stressful family triangle and emotional field, a cascade of healthy shifts ricocheted throughout the family. My mother had more reason to negotiate effectively with Dad when I stopped functioning as a reluctant third party in their decisions. Improved family functions still continue more than a decade later, with a contagion of new energy rippling through networks of in-laws and cousins.

RISING ABOVE FAMILY NORMS

Physical and psychological pain compelled my mother and me to rise above family norms. My tortured back forced me to examine family stress and reach for relief. Anxiety about austere retirement finances pushed my mother into a preemptive strike. In both cases, I see winners throughout the extended family and can identify no losers.

Beyond this situation, my own independent streak has surely jarred my family at other times. But what goes around comes around, and another generation is now ready to choose between conviction or conformity.

Within the past month, my seventeen-year-old son—quite diplomatically, I am pleased to report—advised his dad and me that it can be frustrating to have such conservative parents!

Given conscience-driven deviation from my roots, I don't think of myself as a fall-off-the-map conservative. Thus my shock! Too conservative? What nerve!

Hibernating briefly to ruminate, I realized he's a chip off the old block. Questioning. A seeker. Searching to know himself and to find his own way, not satisfied to be a clone of his parents, a false personality jammed into someone else's mold.

None of us can know God perfectly, so we cannot convey him flawlessly. *What, if any, miscues from my husband or me would prod either of our children away from God?*

Based on my own values, that would be the ultimate tragedy.

I soon found myself responding to my son's declaration. As I write more clearly than I speak, I decided to put my thoughts into a letter. Part of that note to him said:

It's not possible to label God as either conservative or liberal—at least evidence could be used either way. Tamar, who seduced her rascal, betraying father-in-law and bore his child, is portrayed as a heroine and is Jesus' great-great . . . grandmother, as is Rahab "the harlot." Deborah agreed to lead the general into battle (a prophetess, like portable radar) but announced that a woman, not he, would grab the glory of winning the battle (equal rights). Moses married an African, and when his sister, Miriam, mocked him, God struck her with leprosy (interracial marriage). God is big on rescuing and financing the poor: All liberal stuff conservatives tend to ignore. So, for the record, if you gag on conservatives . . . don't blame God. Which brings me to my point:

While I have a responsibility as your mother to exercise my best judgment in guiding you, my radar may, in fact, be far off how God chooses to lead your life. That could prove very different from anything I choose—perhaps to your relief and delight and perhaps to my shock.

PERILS OF COERCION

Some faith-based families might prefer to whack kids with biblical concepts of family hierarchy and "honor thy father and mother" in order to coerce conformity. But consideration of the following factors suggests that alternative tactics not only protect parent-child relations but also create general family well-being.

First, the Creator apparently didn't wire humans for peak

function under coercive conditions. Research shows that extreme parental control can be linked to patterns of schizophrenia, panic attacks, academic failure, and development of

TAKING THIS PERSONALLY . . .
THE PERFECTLY CALIBRATED PERSONALITY

Where, oh where, is the perfectly calibrated personality that never ever, shifts into overcontrol gear? No such saint indwells this skin! The challenge here is not to achieve perfect relationships but to keep mind and heart open to others' subtle or blazing signals to "Back off!" "Cool it!" or "Give me oxygen!"

But we *all* (including, sad to say, my children) descend from flawed personalities. None of us navigate with fail-safe radar. We all misfire at times. And might does *not* always make right.

I occasionally remind my kids that they have not only the privilege, but also perhaps the responsibility to *go over my head.* When convinced I am wrong to inflict punishment or withhold reward, they can

- Appeal to maternal reason (seek Mom's capitulation)
- Negotiate (seek a compromise)
- Go right to the top and seek God's wisdom

"I am a very good reason for you to get to know God," I say. "I will make mistakes, count on it. And you may pay a price when I blow it. But you have a backup plan. So use it. Ask God for guidance and help, even with *moi.*"

There have been many decisions my kids didn't like. At some points, they prayed for relief and voilà!—a surprising solution developed to the delight of all. We realized that

- it pays at times to respectfully and diplomatically go over the heads of mere mortal controllers, and
- sometimes the weaker party may actually be right.

Remembering these points offers great grief relief, rescuing well-intentioned controllers as well as the controlled from pain inflicted by bungled power.

physically and emotionally abusive personalities. Severe personality disorders that derail lives, sabotage jobs, splinter families, and fill prisons are also tied to harshly rigid family environments. Such is the payoff when parental direction and discipline are polluted by excessive control.

Second, faith-driven families can find cues for a balanced blend of warmth, restraint, and resolve directly from scriptural texts that align with the family-transforming strategies presented here. We'll look at a few of the many relevant biblical passages:

- **Transforming Habit: Warm your heart through nurturing relationships.** Surrogate relationships that provided emotional refuge, companionship, and strength are featured throughout biblical texts. Consider David and Jonathan (1 Samuel 18:1-4); Ruth and Naomi (Ruth 1); Elisha and "Mrs. Hospitality" (2 Kings 4:8-37); Jesus and his disciples (John 20:19-20); and Jesus, Mary, Martha, and Lazarus (John 11:1-44).

- **Transforming Habit: Explore and resolve wounds from family history.** "You intended to harm me, but God intended it all for good. He brought me to this position so I could save the lives of many people," said Joseph to his brothers, who had first plotted to kill him before selling him into slavery (Genesis 50:20, NLT). Contemplating the vindictive acts of his hate-filled siblings, Joseph concluded that their vengeance had actually worked to his advantage, launching him into stellar political success, power, and wealth. The revised autobiography in his mind soothed his emotions and helped restore family relationships.

- **Transforming Habit: Find reason to celebrate, even in your grief.** As an infant, Moses was targeted by Pharaoh's order of mass infanticide to eliminate potential rebellion of Hebrew slaves (Exodus 1:22–2:6). Moses escaped death when seized as an adopted son by Pharaoh's daughter. But this trauma to his family offered multiple silver linings evident only with the passage of time:

  1. His mother was hired back as his nanny (Exodus 2:7-8).
  2. Moses' mother earned wages for nurturing her own son—from the very family that had plotted his murder (Exodus 2:9).
  3. Moses transitioned into the royal household as an older boy, gaining an intimate view of the ruling dynasty's culture, judgment, religion, assets, and liabilities—invaluable intelligence for his future mission to emancipate his own people (Exodus 2:10).
  4. Astute in the majority population culture, Moses was primed to win support of palace insiders and Egyptian masses (Exodus 11:3).
  5. Guided by elite Egyptian education, Moses gained negotiating savvy essential in winning ultimate liberation concessions from a ruthless regime (Exodus 12:30-42).

- **Transforming Habit: Define your own role in your extended and nuclear family.** Assigned the role of

family flunky, David refused to accept that label
(1 Samuel 17:12-58). Defying demands of his scornful
brothers, this future king of Israel rose to military
heroism and the head-of-state status for which he
was destined.

- **Transforming Habit: Minimize the family tyrant's
power over you.** Israel's king Saul retaliated with
violence when his son Jonathan rejected a murder
conspiracy against David, a perceived political rival
(1 Samuel 20:16-23). Jonathan chose physical distance,
strong surrogate alliances, and faith to insulate himself
from his father's influence and wrath.

- **Transforming Habit: Seek one-on-one relationships
with each member of your family.** It was bad enough
that Jacob favored his son, Joseph, but Joseph flaunted
his superiority in ways that drove his brothers to a
fratricidal scheme against him. It was a good thing
Joseph's diplomatic brother, Judah, had established
relations with all factions in the family. Judah's
connections and appeal enabled him to negotiate a
compromise, saving Joseph's life (Genesis 37:26-28).
The payoff for the bloodthirsty brothers was that the
sibling they spared later rescued them from misery and
possible starvation. Destiny for this violent, scheming
family first hinged on the family's diplomatic
prodigy—Judah, *not* his famed little brother.

- **Transforming Habit: Embrace a vibrant connection
with God.** Consider David. Minimized, even scorned
by his family, embroiled in palace intrigue, and targeted

for annihilation by political enemies, David found emotional relief, courage, hope, and inspiration from his sense of a remarkably intimate relationship with God, as expressed throughout Psalms.

- **Transforming Habit: Exercise judicious generosity.** The father described in Luke 15:11-32 shared wealth with his son, who then ran off, squandered the dough, and slid into homeless squalor as he literally moved to a pigsty. The father did not pursue his prodigal son to rescue him from self-inflicted misery. Nor did Dad bribe his son to reform, pull strings for a cushy job, or even ease the journey home. Such injudicious giving would have insulated this son from the self-inflicted misery that generated greater wisdom, better judgment, and the good sense to return to a generous but judicious father eager to give him another chance.

CONCLUSION

The principles we've explored in this book draw heavily upon the respected work of pioneers in family therapy and have been validated by the inspiring successes of many clients. We've also seen how a vibrant faith can transform family despair into hope, life energy, and achievement.

Truly, there are many times I could shout for joy (I restrain myself) when I see the victories savored by those who successfully employ these principles. May you and those in your life share that experience, finding gratification in your own adventure with family-transforming concepts.

TEST YOUR FAMILY TRANSFORMATION IQ

WHICH RESPONSE WOULD YOU CHOOSE?

Situations in the cases described below often have several possible solutions. Plans that work with some personalities and families would produce disaster in others. Options are explored here to clarify difficulties and describe how some solutions have produced relief for family pain. Consider how the following choices might work for you, or what improvements you might make for success in your own situation.

■ ■ ■

Case 1: Intrusive Mother/Mother-in-Law

We'll start with a true personal story. I asked my son when he was about fourteen, "When you're say, thirty-five, suppose I come to visit your home. Maybe by then you will have a wife and children. I watch awhile, then say, 'Here are some behaviors you should change with your wife and children and better ways to run your home.' How should you respond?"

His response was one of the following choices. Which would you choose—or would you give a completely different response?

A. Reply, "Thanks, Mom, but I'm able to manage my own home my way."

B. Tell your mother, "Your bossy days are over, Mom. Just knock it off!"

C. Nod and agree to keep peace, then do as you please.

Seeing so much pain among clients whose extended families show no respect for boundaries, I wanted to give my son an edge just in case a more crotchety me someday makes a similar mistake. He immediately—and very respectfully—responded, unprompted, with option A: "Thanks, Mom, but I'm able to manage my own home my way!"

Chuckling with delight at my son's healthy independence, I responded: "Yes! You'd owe it to your wife and kids not to allow such intrusion. But just remember," I added quietly, "I *am* your mother. So be gentle!"

A family-functioning issue to consider: a confused hierarchy is created when parents abdicate proper authority in their own home or when their executive functions are eroded by outsiders, as I could do in the scenario described with my son.

■ ■ ■

Case 2: Budget-Busting Ivy Leaguer

Jeremy demanded that his parents pay for him to attend an expensive Ivy League university, but his parents had saved enough only to cover tuition at a much less expensive state university for their two sons. Jeremy heatedly accused them of ruining his future opportunities for success, and his parents were torn as they lurched from rage at his selfishness to guilt for their failure to bankroll his dreams. What should they have done?

A. Stuck to Plan A: Informed Jeremy that they'd pay for the reasonable state university or he was on his own.

B. Agreed to clean out their savings for Jeremy's dream school, hoping it wouldn't risk the family's future too much.

C. Offered the money earmarked for Jeremy to either finance most of a state university program or finance a fraction of the Ivy League tuition—his call.

All-or-nothing thinking shows up frequently in families, which prevents them from exploring solutions sensitive to the concerns of all. Decades after college, some adults whose parents forced them against their will to attend colleges they disliked (option A) still simmer with resentment for being denied a voice on a major decision that affects the rest of their life. Option C offers a win-win solution: The child wins the privilege of attending a higher priced college *if* he or she can generate the extra funds needed (and many succeed in this challenge). The parents win protection of their economic security but often also win gratitude for honoring a young adult's dreams. A family-functioning issue to consider: Reciprocity—that is, mutual influence and consideration—is a key predictor of successful family functioning.

■ ■ ■

Case 3: A Shark of a Father-in-Law

Mr. Smith owned a seafood restaurant managed by his son, Wally. Mr. Smith frequently invited Wally's wife, Bess, to join them for an early dinner. But Mr. Smith also frequently launched dinner tirades against Wally, charging that he managed by incompetence, idiocy, and laziness. Bess wanted to maintain cordial relations with her father-in-law but detested these scenes that were so humiliating to her husband. What were her options?

A. Turn down all future dinner invitations from her father-in-law.

B. Advise Wally that at the next such scene, she would quietly call a taxi and go home with him or without him, as he preferred.

C. Ask her father-in-law to drop his crude behavior.

Bess considered telling her husband to get the backbone to stand up to his abusive father but then realized she'd be just like her father-in-law: a bossy voice of ridicule. She chose plan B—respecting her husband's right to choose for himself but deciding that she would quietly excuse herself the next time her father-in-law became abrasive. With husband Wally's prior knowledge, she executed her plan, prompting a discussion with her father-in-law. Wally spoke up and warned that he, too, would leave any future family scene of verbal abuse. Wally's dad was startled that for once relatives confronted his abuse, and he actually apologized. Relief rippled through the entire family as the patriarch got a grip on himself—thanks to Bess's thoughtful courage. An issue to consider: Family warmth, a predictor of positive functions within and outside the home, is depleted by personalities like Wally's dad at grave risk to the family.

■ ■ ■

Case 4: Baby Brothers . . . for How Long?
Sally had a steady job with modest wages but budgeted strictly and socked away savings for security. Her younger, capable but unreliable brothers were erratically employed, constantly cashless, and repeatedly at her door for money. She should have:

A. Given them enough to send them packing but not enough to drain her savings.

B. Told them never, ever to ask for money again, after so many handouts.

C. Offered to pay them only if they did a good job washing her car, mowing her lawn, and tackling other chores she planned to pay someone to do anyway.

"Dependency in physically healthy adults is pathological— it is sick, always a manifestation of a mental illness or defect," notes M. Scott Peck in *The Road Less Traveled.*[1] Despite many biblical directives to respond generously to the poor, Peck's tough love also is rooted in biblical concepts: "If a man will not work, he shall not eat," declares 2 Thessalonians 3:10. Responding to such values, Sally chose option C, offering to pay her brothers for jobs but noting that their freeloading days were over. An issue to consider: Overresponsibility by any family member tends to breed underresponsibility in others.

■ ■ ■

Case 5: Blind Rage

In their seventies, a man and his wife had worked hard to save about two hundred thousand dollars each over long years of earning modest wages. For years, the husband had very faithfully managed his wife's money, as she was in poor health and nearly blind. But she was a very suspicious type and constantly accused him of stealing her money, mostly because she forgot where she put the small stashes she'd stuffed in secret spots around the house. Old and weak himself, the man was getting tired of the constant accusations. What should he have done?

A. Told his wife, "You're a definite dingbat if you can't remember where you hid your own money!"

B. Ignored the constant blame he'd already survived for fifty years.

C. Told her, "You have three choices when it comes to money: You can manage your money yourself, you can get the bank or an accountant to manage it, or you can let me manage it, but only if you stop all the accusations. If you choose the third option, you must understand that I'll turn over this job to someone else the next time you accuse me of mismanagement."

Sadly, this man chose option B—to forever tolerate his wife's accusations. But as they grew elderly and sick, they weren't even speaking to each other except when absolutely necessary. This man was very bitter that for his loyalty and dedication, he'd gotten years of verbal abuse. But he refused to correct his own passive responses. What if he had many years earlier chosen option C: to turn over his wife's money management to a trusted third party if she continued assaulting his character and wounding his spirit? Based on similar cases, I believe she was more likely to control herself than seek an outside money manager—*if she believed her husband would enforce his declaration.* A family-functioning issue to consider: Healthy self-esteem could have reduced decades of marital pain if this husband had respected himself enough to refuse emotional abuse by his wife. As implied by Jesus in Matthew 22:39, love for ourselves is a prerequisite for loving others.

■ ■ ■

Case 6: Brewed Sister

Bart bought a car for his seventy-year-old mother to use, and it was covered by his insurance. But she lived with Bart's alcohol-abusing, car-crashing sister, and over Bart's protests his mother let the sister drive the car even if she'd been drinking. Bart's fear was his liability if the sister crashed in his car. What should Bart have done?

A. Transferred the car title and insurance from Bart's name to his mother's name.

B. Advised his mother that if the sister used the car again, Bart would sell the car and make other transportation arrangements for his mother.

C. Written his sister a notarized letter, documenting an order for her not to use the car.

If Bart or his mother had been sued because his drinking, demolition-derby sister maimed or killed someone by a car owned and insured by one of them, they would not have been victims—they would have been volunteers. They would have known the risks in advance, so they also would have shared guilt in any destruction to others. After warning his mother and learning that his sister had gotten behind the wheel again, Bart sold the car (option B) and arranged for an elder-care driving service to drive his mother around town. In this way he still guaranteed his mother's mobility without putting others in danger or himself at risk. An issue to consider: Judicious giving *improves* individual and family functions, while injudicious giving can perpetuate pain. A good question to ask before pursuing internal family charity: *Will my gift help this relative function better or more responsibly without creating new problems or reinforcing old ones?*

■ ■ ■

Case 7: You Want This Guy in the Chromosome Pool?

A twenty-five-year-old woman was engaged to a thirty-year-old man who'd had his driver's license revoked. She drove him to and from work every day, meeting him at his job at 6 PM for the trip home as they had agreed. Night after night, he dragged himself to the car sometime between 6:45 and 8:30 PM, regardless of her complaints. Since she was determined to stick with the relationship, what should this woman have done?

A. Advised him of a new policy: When he didn't arrive by 6:10 PM she'd leave him to find his own way home.
B. Begged his mother to set him straight.
C. More forcefully denounced his rudeness, ingratitude, and selfishness when he was late.

Here's the problem with option B: Such triangulation pulls in third parties (the mother) in an attempt to pressure someone to change (the fiancé). But triangulation tends to backfire, expanding and intensifying conflict and perpetuating an inability to work out differences adult to adult. This young woman chose option A, driving off one day after waiting for ten minutes. The fiancé called in anger, but she said, "From now on, you've got ten minutes. If you're a no-show, I go." For the brief period I observed, the fiancé was more punctual . . . but his selfish habits were not a positive predictor for the pending marriage. A family-functioning issue to consider: Autonomy or self-direction resists unjust or unfair conditions imposed by self-indulgent, exploiting personalities.

■ ■ ■

Case 8: Man or Munchkin?
D. S. Jesse showed up for a death-defying competitive event where his older brothers ridiculed him as the family squirt.

They ordered him to leave the event to real men and run home to Dad. Actually, the clan hadn't observed the risky competitions D. S. had already won, and now he wanted a shot at this high-profile event. What should he have done?

A. Exited gracefully to avoid embarrassing the family.
B. Calculated his odds for success and then competed based on that judgment, regardless of family pecking order or old role assignments.
C. Publicly challenged his arrogant brothers to a test of manhood.

I threw in this example to make the point that some things never change, including family dysfunctions: If D. S. Jesse (David, son of Jesse, 1 Samuel 17:17-58) had embraced his family's role for himself, this shepherd boy would have hung out with the sheep while humongous Goliath turned David's resentful brothers into hamburger. Deflecting disdainful external controllers, David responded to a national crisis using his own conscience, judgment, and skill (option B). David, his family, and his nation would have risked massive losses had he failed to override external forces with internal direction. An issue to consider: Chosen roles can tap into an individual's gifts, expertise, and internal sense of direction, while roles imposed by family members often disregard such factors.

■ ■ ■

Case 9: Sonny Days—More or Less?

The state of Arkansas threw Phil, thirty-two, in jail for marijuana possession, then gave him a one-way ticket home to

Washington, D.C., promising to arrest him immediately if he set foot in the state again. Mama, sixty-two, took him in, but had neither the energy nor the cash to perpetually rescue this beloved son. She should have:

A. Told him that if he used drugs again, he was going to be out on the street.

B. Let him stay if he assumed household chores.

C. Taken him to the local mission for their demanding yearlong residential rehabilitation program.

Drug abusers often admit that their recovery really began on the day that Mom or spouse finally set limits, with option C cited as a smart move by grateful sons at Washington's Gospel Rescue Ministries. The drug abuser, of course, can choose not to enter the rehab program. But Mama, likewise, can choose not to run an eternal bed-and-breakfast (over-responsibility) for an adult child given to self-destructive life habits (underresponsibility). An issue to consider: Transition to adult-to-adult relations between parents and their grown children requires that children cease childlike dependence and that parents resist debilitating coddling of another adult.

■ ■ ■

Case 10: One or Two Truly Blue?
Because he refused to take his medicine regularly, Gary suffered severe mood swings that made him a miserable companion. After twenty years, Cecelia was determined to stay in

the marriage but wanted relief from Gary's self-inflicted misery. She should have:

A. Filled her life with stimulating interests and nurturing people to dilute her daily dosage of moody Gary.

B. Holed up at her home office in an attempt to stay away from him.

C. Secretly put his medicine into his food.

Taking Solomon's advice to protect her own mental health by minimizing time with a grouch (Proverbs 22:24-25), Cecelia returned to full-time employment (option A). This way she could be productive, enhance family income, and tolerate a lower daily dose of Gary, but keep her family intact. Even Gary seemed happier with an arrangement that gave him less opportunity for marital conflict. An issue to consider: The inevitable mind-relationship linkage assures that moody habits by either marital partner risk both partners and their marital cohesion, while squelching family warmth essential for nurturing the emotional life of parents and children.

■ ■ ■

Case 11: One Agitated Granny

"Can you sit with the kids tonight?" David asked his seventy-five-year-old mother.

"Same old, same old," she muttered later as she cancelled bingo plans with her neighbor to once again rescue her son. "He always calls at the last minute, ruins my plans, and never gives me the time of day except as a sitter," she complained.

This grandma wanted to maintain a relationship with her son but would have appreciated a bit of consideration and respect. What should she have done?

    A. Set terms for child care: "Call a week ahead, and I can usually come through. But if I get last-minute calls, I'm not going to cancel my plans with friends."

    B. Turned him down several times so he'd appreciate her more.

    C. Taken the grandkids to bingo.

Here's the pattern: Elderly folks who gripe and complain about being taken for granted often 1) continue to be exploited while 2) driving others away. Part of the problem is often mixed signals: Grandma says, "Bring over the grandkids anytime," but she's mad when this happens. Some of my clients have finally learned in their sixties and seventies to clarify their limits and expect common courtesy (option A), earning new freedom and respect from their younger relations. An issue to consider: Authenticity is a prerequisite for emotional intimacy, while "faking it" to please others brews resentment, erodes trust, and often leads to a major relational meltdown.

■ ■ ■

Case 12: Holiday Hog

Midwesterners Cherry and Jim had parents on opposite sides of the continent: California and New Jersey. Cherry insisted on taking her husband and two kids to her parents' every

Christmas, dismissing her husband's desire for equal Yule time with his family. Jim should have:

A. Boycotted the in-law Christmas trip and stayed home.

B. Contrary to old patterns, made plans to take the children every other Christmas to his parents, inviting Cherry, of course.

C. Capitulated to his wife's demands for "peace at any cost."

Research shows that men who refuse to be influenced by their wife's desires have an 81 percent chance of an imploding marriage.[2] But a wife who behaves like a drill sergeant generates misery as well. My challenge to the passive victim is inevitably to summon the courage and integrity for a diplomatic shift similar to option B: more shared decision making. This is risky, as drill sergeants are shocked when their silent partners finally find a voice. But permanent capitulation (option C) is also hazardous—as discovered too late by the elderly husband in case 5, whose dormant posture was spirit-shriveling, embittering, and alienating. Peril also builds as the controlling partner loses respect for a spaghetti-spine mate exhibiting such a dull inner life. Sometimes a client seeks more shared power in a lopsided marriage, only to learn that his or her own silence was the biggest problem. The sometimes unintentional controller cannot read minds, and the victim's unspoken wishes can be totally off the partner's radar. An issue to consider: Buried beneath every frustration is a hidden desire, which must be clearly spoken before the responsiveness of a partner can be truly judged.

■ ■ ■

Case 13: Exiled

Max was shocked early in his marriage when his wife, Gloria, announced: "Your father can never visit this house again!" While visiting from five states away, Max's father had told Gloria she sure could lose a few pounds, and for that he was permanently banished. Max saw the punishment as too extreme for the offense, but for twenty-five years he agreed to Gloria's demands to avoid her anger. Now that his father was elderly and sick, Max felt very guilty. He wanted to invite his father, a World War II veteran, to visit overnight and share local Memorial Day festivities. What should Max have done?

A. Asked Gloria for permission to break her "no visit" rule.
B. Announced that his father was visiting, whether she liked it or not.
C. Forgotten about inviting his father, but visited him instead.

It wasn't just that Gloria resented Max's indiscreet father. She didn't like his mother either. Or his siblings. Or for that matter even her own siblings. Nor could she keep friends for long. She seemed to have deeply rooted feelings of inferiority, and any relationship that failed to soothe her shaky ego felt hostile, including her marriage. She constantly shoved Max away and then blamed him for distance.

While he truly loved his mercurial wife, Max felt deep sorrow that other relatives he also loved were deeply wounded by his choices. He chose a compromise between options A and B: Max advised his wife that he was inviting his dad for the

Memorial Day weekend. (Message: *I am exercising adult decision making without granting veto power.*)

He said he would be very pleased if she would share some or all of the weekend with them. (Message: *You are valued and desired here.*)

He also announced his plan to take all responsibility for weekend food and entertainment. (Message: *I am choosing for myself but am not dumping demands on you.*)

Max anticipated resentment of his decision by his wife, an emotional blackmailer who unleashed anger, blame, and rejection when people veered from her demands. Despite another dose of Gloria's anger, Max felt better in his own skin as his moral compass was reactivated. An issue to consider: Nondefensive communication with emotional blackmailers can improve personal decision making and minimize conflict.[3]

Max achieved this by:

- Explaining his decision without apologizing for himself or blaming his wife.
- Anticipating and preparing for her likely responses— assuming he would entertain his dad.
- Tolerating his wife's resentment without getting sucked into either anger or resentment in return. (He stayed out of her emotional field.)

■ ■ ■

Case 14: The Accuser
Whenever Molly returned home from weekend trips with her church youth group for skiing, missions programs, or summer

conferences, her mother welcomed her home with the same question: "Who did you sleep with?" In fact, one boy in the youth group *was* very attractive to Molly, and they had shared a secret with each other and with their small group of church friends: They had all made a "no sex before marriage" pact.

To be accused of a behavior that was offensive to her own moral code insulted and angered Molly. *"You are just nuts!"* she screamed at her mother. *"You accuse me of this over and over, and I'm sick of it!"* The mother then screamed back, called her husband for backup, and both parents chastised Molly for her "disrespect," "tantrums," and "insults to your mother!" What should Molly have done?

A. Refused to speak to her parents until they apologized.

B. Declined to go on any more youth group trips.

C. Asked her mother: "What have I ever done to justify such accusations?"

This mother's mind was quicksand for her teenage daughter. The mother nurtured a mental image of a sexually indulgent teenager, which then compelled Molly to respond to a mental image of herself that she found insulting. Revolted by an image superimposed upon her, Molly reacted in anger, spiraling into a trap. Now she was not only viewed as morally deficient but parent-maligning as well, damaging her image in the mind of her father, who exhibited affection for Molly until baited by the mother-daughter conflict. To avoid more damage to her heart and spirit, Molly needed to understand several realities.

False accusations were a form of abusive speech that invaded her boundaries and did violence to her spirit, regardless of the source.

Two tips from Solomon could have saved her grief: "A gentle answer turns away wrath, but a harsh word stirs up anger" (Proverbs 15:1) and "He who guards his mouth and his tongue keeps himself from calamity" (Proverbs 21:23).

Molly took Solomon's advice to censor her own speech and planned a calm, thoughtful, respectful response to her mother's next accusation. Molly used questions as her answers:

Molly: Mom, how many times have you asked me this question?

Mother (contemplated, then spoke quietly): Many times.

Molly: My answer is always the same, because this is who I am. When you accuse me of this stuff, I pull away from you. So can you please agree not to ask this same question again unless you have some kind of evidence that I've changed my mind? And that is not going to happen!

Her mother was silent, but the accusations ceased.

An issue to consider: Recognizing verbal abuse is a first step in protecting both self and family from toxic speech. *The Verbally Abusive Relationship* by Patricia Evans offers strategies for squelching your own verbal-abuse tendencies and those in your family.[4]

■ ■ ■

Case 15: Patriarch Pain

Since Virginia's spry seventy-year-old father had moved into her family's basement bedroom eight months before, tension in the family had soared. Grandpa contradicted Virginia when she was enforcing rules with her two teenagers, criticized Virginia as a working mom whose meals and housekeeping didn't meet his standards, and inevitably butted into marital disputes to take sides with his son-in-law. Thanks to her father, Virginia felt increasingly on the defensive and alienated from her own children and husband. What should she have done?

A. As this was a failed experiment and her dad had money to live elsewhere, ejected Grandpa from her household.

B. Enacted policies that protected relationships with her husband and children as well as with her father.

C. Respected the patriarch's right to dominate the household.

Elderly parents who move in with their middle-aged children confront multiple traps. They're often disappointed with the poor companionship offered by their children and grandchildren, who are consumed by jobs and school. These elders also generally feel a loss of freedom and social connections, as well as confusion about their role in the family. The middle-generation female feels added stress, caught between demands of older and younger generations and those of her spouse. Privacy is lost as the adults tend to poke into each other's business, and family warmth can plummet overnight. Virginia chose to identify and pursue desires of all family members (option B), which could have saved her grief if explored *before* Grandpa ever moved in.

For example, Grandpa wanted clarity on expectations for

him and also more social life outside the family, where he felt freer to be himself.

Virginia wanted one dinner a week just with her husband and children and one dinner a week just with her husband, to sustain connections that seemed strained when conversation was diverted by Grandpa's many opinions.

The children wanted two bosses, not three.

Virginia's husband wanted his wife back—more time without distractions from the children and Grandpa.

An issue to consider: Those who fail to define their own role in the family will have others define it for them.

DISCUSSION GUIDE

Chapter 1: All in the Family

1. Based on Harvard's Study of Adult Development, how do you think the *loveless* home of Bonnie and Bobby helps explain their tormented journey as young adults?

2. If they had been *cherished* children, how might their adult relationships and quality of life have been different?

3. If your family features a Jekyll and Hyde character—publicly harmless but privately destructive—how have you been affected emotionally, socially, and spiritually by that relationship?

4. "If anyone says, 'I love God,' yet hates his brother, he is a liar," says 1 John 4:20 (NIV). If a family member talks religiously one moment but the next shows contempt for his or her spouse, children, or others, what does such behavior reveal about that person's core nature? How is the next generation affected emotionally, socially, and spiritually?

5. Consider Ephesians 6:4 (NIV), "Fathers, do not exasperate your children; instead, bring them up in the training and instruction of the Lord." How have adults in your parents' or your own generation aggravated children into angry or rebellious behaviors?

Chapter 2: Wired for Warmth

Transforming Habit: Warm your heart through nurturing relationships.

1. What childhood experiences may explain why Thomas Lincoln became a harsh and punishing father to his son—future U.S. president Abraham Lincoln? In what ways did suffering in Abe's early life perhaps shape him as a giant force for good?

2. In what four ways did Bonnie transform her battered heart into a safe refuge for her husband and children?

3. During the past week, in what specific ways have you demonstrated the four family warmth factors cited in this chapter? During the next week, how can you measure your own progress on each factor?

4. Considering the following as examples of surrogate family, in what ways do you think these connected personalities were mutual sources of warmth or empowerment?
   David and Jonathan (1 Samuel 18:1-4; 19–20)
   Esther and her maidservants (Esther 4:15-16)
   Ruth and her mother-in-law, Naomi (Ruth 1:3-19)
   Jesus and the three siblings, Mary, Martha, and Lazarus (John 11:1-44)

5. Name and briefly describe a surrogate relationship—substitute family—that has given you emotional warmth, hope, strength, courage, or safe refuge. How would your life have been different without that relationship?

Chapter 3: Mourning Losses

Transforming Habit: Explore and resolve wounds from family history.

1. What destructive family behaviors could Micah trace back many generations to the American slave era, when wounds were inflicted from outside the family? How did Micah seek to reverse painful multigenerational patterns?

2. How have the following people contributed to pain in your own life?
   Parents
   Grandparents
   Generations prior to grandparents, or extended family (siblings, aunts, uncles)
3. How did these four generations (Abraham, Isaac, Jacob, Joseph) suffer from family habits of favoritism, betrayal, and treachery? Regarding family treachery, which characters were instigators, coconspirators, or victims? Why do you think the next generation inflicted the same old family pain?
   Abraham-Sarah (Genesis 21:8-10, 14-16)
   Isaac-Rebekah (Genesis 27:5-45)
   Jacob-sons (Genesis 37:2-4, 18-28)
4. What painful habits in your family can you reject for yourself? Who are you willing to recruit as a confidant to help you honor this commitment for the next six months?

Chapter 4: Celebrate and Embrace Good Grief
Transforming Habit: Find reason to celebrate, even in your grief.
1. Sharon assumed that she was a big loser because her parents greatly favored her sister, Christine. What evidence did Sharon discover that proved she wasn't such a loser after all? When Sharon's family beliefs changed, how did her emotions, behaviors, relationships, and quality of life also change?
2. How did Dr. Herbert Benson explain his confused memories as triggers for physical reactions of sweat, nausea, and rapid heart rate?
3. Prominent Nazi death camp survivor Viktor Frankl describes personal qualities that seemed to predict survival. Which of these mental, emotional, and behavioral habits have you used—*or can you now use*—to overcome pain in your own history?
4. Sold by his brothers into slavery, Joseph rose to a supreme political position in his adopted land of Egypt. Of his remarkable journey from slavery to power, Joseph later declared to his brothers, "Don't be angry with yourselves for selling me to this place. It was God who sent me here ahead of you to preserve your lives" (Genesis 45:5, NLT). How can you also celebrate gains in your life that have come through pain—including improved factors below?

Character	Vision
Perseverance	Wisdom
Faith	Compassion
Drive	Opportunity

Chapter 5: Activate a Family Freedom Formula
Transforming Habit: Define your own role in your extended and nuclear family.
1. In what ways did Jesse's mother impose risky roles on her thirty-three-year-old, six-foot-three, bodybuilder, ex-con son? How did Jesse encourage his mother's childlike dependence on him?

2. What risky roles *have you accepted* in your nuclear or extended families? What unhealthy roles *have you imposed* on your parents, siblings, spouse, or children?

3. As seen in the chapter 3 study guide, Rebekah recruited her favorite son, Jacob, for roles of family betrayer and exploiter. Meanwhile, she reduced his twin, Esau, to an emotional and financial victim. The brothers reconciled decades later when both rejected destructive family roles. Describe steps taken by each brother for reconciliation:

   Jacob (Genesis 31:3; 32:3-8, 13-21; 33:3, 8-15)
   Esau (Genesis 33:4-9, 12-15)

4. In what ways can you take each step of this chapter's Family Freedom Formula to choose healthier family roles?

Chapter 6: Taming Family Tyrants

Transforming Habit: Minimize the family tyrant's power over you.

1. As publisher of the *Washington Post*, Katharine Graham seemed hard as nails when her challenges sent U.S. president Richard Nixon careening into history. But in her marriage, what behaviors did she tolerate that showed a much more vulnerable side to her nature?

2. How does a cyclical family abuser use some of the external decision-making tools cited in this chapter to control victims?

3. How do multigenerational behavior patterns produce abusive personalities?

4. As described in this chapter and 1 Samuel 25, what external and internal assets did Abigail use to minimize destruction by her explosive spouse? How can you better use such external and internal assets to stabilize your own family?

5. From this chapter, how can you specifically apply Nehemiah's Family-Legacy Recovery Formula (Nehemiah 9) for relief from family wounders and tyrants?

Chapter 7: Reach for Connection

Transforming Habit: Seek one-on-one relationships with each member of your family.

1. In what ways did family adulterer Wade and his wife, Lana, both sabotage their marriage and the emotional safety of their children? How did the grown children imitate the destructive relationship habits of their parents?

2. Back to the Jacob-Esau reconciliation focus of the chapter 5 study guide (see Genesis 31–33 readings). How did these estranged brothers apply principles like those in this chapter's Family-Peacemaker Strategy to recover from decades of alienation? How can you apply the Family-Peacemaker Strategy to develop warmer and safer one-on-one relationships in your own family?

3. Describe how two or more positive relationships outside your family have been gifts in your life. When you think of these heart-warmers, how have you absorbed any of the positive surrogate qualities suggested in this chapter? This week, pause to thank them and/or thank God for the ways they have blessed your life.

Chapter 8: WOW! Faith Families

Transforming Habit: Embrace a vibrant connection with God.

1. How did behavior changes by single mom Sonja Carson and her son, Ben, catapult him

from poverty and failure to status as Johns Hopkins' world-renowned pediatric neurosurgeon?

2. How did personalized faith in teenagers Ben Carson and Emily seem to impact:
   Emotional stability
   Judgment
   Relationships
   Hope or opportunity
3. According to research, how does faith produce advantages in:
   Teen stability and achievement
   Marital satisfaction
   Health
4. What choices can you make to avoid the three faith traps described in the concluding section of this chapter?
5. Jesus expressed amazement at the simple but powerful faith of the Roman military officer described in Luke 7:1-10. Like Ben and Emily, his focus was not so much on organized religion but on his belief that God offers such a personal relationship with each of us that he responds directly to our private concerns. How does your faith focus on a personal connection to God, and how does it focus on the officials and guidelines of organizations?
6. Jesus promised that faith can propel people beyond overwhelming obstacles (Matthew 17:20; Mark 5:24-34; Luke 7:6-10). For the next six months, on what emotional, relational, financial, or physical challenges are you willing to seek daily help from God—and see what develops?

Chapter 9: My Family's Transformation

Transforming Habit: Exercise judicious generosity.

1. How did the author perpetuate unwise financial habits in her family of origin? How had her family assigned her the role of financial rescuer?
2. What steps did the author take to reverse her own behaviors that contributed to family pain? How did changing her old family role seem to trigger new choices by other family members?
3. When the Prodigal Son squandered family money and slid into a debauched lifestyle (Luke 15:11-32), his father did not chase after him, coddle, beg, or coerce him into conformity to family values. How do you think this father's restrained responses might have had a different effect on the son's decision making than a more forceful father's reaction might have had?
4. How does your family respond to members who reject family values? What can you learn from the Prodigal Son and his father about maintaining personal integrity and making thoughtful decisions while protecting relationships in your family?

ENDNOTES

INTRODUCTION
1. Oliver Sacks, *The Man Who Mistook His Wife for a Hat* (New York: Summit Books, 1985).
2. Patricia D. Roth, "Spiritual Well-Being and Marital Adjustment," *Journal of Psychology and Theology* 16, no. 2 (1988): 153–158.
3. John G. Gunderson and Alex N. Sabo, "The Phenomenological and Conceptual Interface between Borderline Personality Disorder and PTSD," *American Journal of Psychiatry* 150, no. 1 (1993): 19–27.
4. George Vaillant, *Aging Well: Surprising Guideposts to a Happier Life from the Landmark Harvard Study of Adult Development* (Boston: Little, Brown and Company, 2002).

CHAPTER 1: All in the Family
1. George Vaillant, *Aging Well: Surprising Guideposts to a Happier Life from the Landmark Harvard Study of Adult Development* (Boston: Little, Brown and Company, 2002), 94–100.

CHAPTER 2: Wired for Warmth
1. This and preceding quotes on Lincoln come from William E. Gienapp, *Abraham Lincoln and Civil War America: A Biography* (New York: Oxford Press, 2002), 4.
2. Sharon Begley, "How to Build a Baby's Brain," *Newsweek* special edition, (Spring/Summer 1997): 28–32.
3. Daniel Goleman, *Emotional Intelligence* (New York: Bantam, 1995), 96–110.

4. C. S. Lewis, *The Four Loves* (New York: A Harvest Book/ Harcourt Brace & Company, 1960).

CHAPTER 3: Mourning Losses

1. Dan Allendar, *The Wounded Heart* (Colorado Springs: NavPress, 1990), 13.

CHAPTER 4: Celebrate and Embrace Good Grief

1. Herbert Benson, *Timeless Healing: The Power and Biology of Belief* (New York: Fireside/Simon & Schuster, 1996), 77.
2. Antonio Damasio, *The Feeling of What Happens: Body and Emotion in the Making of Consciousness* (San Diego: Harvest Book/Harcourt, Inc., 1999), 173–233.
3. Viktor E. Frankl, *Man's Search for Meaning* (New York: Touchtone/Simon & Schuster, 1959), 17, 55.
4. George Engel, "Sudden and Rapid Death during Psychological Stress: Folklore or Folk Wisdom?" *Annals of Internal Medicine* 74 (1971): 771–782. Cited in Benson, *Timeless Healing.*
5. Frankl, *Man's Search for Meaning,* 16–82.
6. M. Scott Peck, *The Road Less Traveled: A New Psychology of Love, Traditional Values and Spiritual Growth* (New York: Touchstone Books/Simon & Schuster, 1978), 290–296.

CHAPTER 5: Activate a Family Freedom Formula

1. Murray Bowen, *Family Therapy in Clinical Practice* (New York: Aronson, 1978), 520, 524.
2. David Burns, *The Feeling Good Handbook* (New York: Plume/ Penguin Group, 1989), 73–96.

CHAPTER 6: Taming Family Tyrants

1. Katharine Graham, *Personal History* (New York: Vintage Books, 1997), 110–111.
2. Graham, *Personal History*, 140.
3. Susan Forward, *Emotional Blackmail* (New York: Harper Collins, 1997), 123–125.
4. Graham, *Personal History,* 213.
5. Graham, *Personal History,* 214, 231.
6. Patricia Evans, *The Verbally Abusive Relationship: How to*

Recognize It and How to Respond (Holbrook, Mass.: Adams Media Corporation, 1996), 60–78.

7. John N. Briere, *Child Abuse Trauma: Theory and Treatment of the Lasting Effects* (Newbury Park, Calif.: SAGE Publications, 1992), 73–76.

8. Donald G. Dutton, *The Abusive Personality: Violence and Control in Intimate Relationships* (New York: The Guilford Press, 1998), 152.

9. Ibid., 141.

10. "Gallup Index of Leading Religious Indicators" (Princeton, N.J.: The Gallup Organization, 2002).

11. Rick Warren, *The Purpose-Driven Life* (Grand Rapids, Mich.: Zondervan, 2002), 193–199.

12. Ibid., 97.

13. Jeffrey J. Magnavita, *Restructuring Personality Disorders* (New York: The Guilford Press, 1997), 218.

14. Judith Mishne, *The Evolution and Application of Clinical Theory: Perspectives from Four Psychologies* (New York: The Free Press/Macmillan, Inc., 1993), 233.

15. Stephanie Donaldson-Pressman and Robert M. Pressman, *The Narcissistic Family: Diagnosis and Treatment* (New York: Lexington Books, 1994), 51–64.

CHAPTER 7: Reach for Connection

1. James L. Framo, *Family-of-Origin Therapy: An Intergenerational Approach* (New York: Brunner/Mazel, 1992), 1.

2. John M. Gottman and Nan Silver, *The Seven Principles for Making Marriage Work* (New York: Three Rivers Press, 1999), 22.

3. Harriet Goldhor Lerner, *The Dance of Intimacy* (New York: Harper & Row, 1989), 85.

4. Murray Bowen, *Family Therapy in Clinical Practice* (New York: Aronson, 1978), 370.

5. Daniel Goleman, *Emotional Intelligence* (New York: Bantam, 1995), 200–214.

6. Wanda M. Malcolm and Leslie S. Greenberg, "Forgiveness as a Process of Change in Individual Psychotherapy," in *Forgiveness: Theory, Research, and Practice,* ed. Michael E.

McCullough et al. (New York: The Guilford Press, 2000), 179–202.

7. Julie Juola Exline and Roy F. Baumeister, "Expressing Forgiveness and Repentance: Benefits and Barriers," in *Forgiveness* (see note 6), 133–155.

8. Gottman and Silver, *Seven Principles for Making Marriage Work*, 27–34.

9. Ibid., 4–5.

10. Herbert Benson, *Timeless Healing* (New York: Fireside/Simon & Schuster, 1996), 49–50.

11. Andrew Weil, *Spontaneous Healing* (New York: Fawcett Columbine/The Ballentine Publishing Group, 2000), 99.

12. See http://www.ivpress.com/spotlight/3244.php.

13. Benson, *Timeless Healing,* 203.

14. William Manchester, *The Last Lion: Winston Spencer Churchill: Visions of Glory, 1874–1932* (Boston: Little, Brown and Company, 1983), 17.

15. Manchester, *The Last Lion*, 168, 223–226, 331, 411–412.

16. Armand M. Nicholi Jr., *The Question of God: C. S. Lewis and Sigmund Freud Debate God, Love, Sex, and the Meaning of Life* (New York: Free Press/Simon & Schuster, Inc., 2002), 29.

17. C. S. Lewis, *Surprised by Joy* (New York: Harvest Book/Harcourt, Inc., 1955), 148.

18. Gina O'Connell Higgins, *Resilient Adults: Overcoming a Cruel Past* (San Francisco: Jossey-Bass Publishers, 1994), 125–169.

CHAPTER 8: WoW! Faith Families

1. Phil McCombs, "The Doctor's Saving Grace," *Washington Post,* 7 August 2002, C01. See also Ben Carson, *Think Big* (Grand Rapids, Mich.: Zondervan, 1992) and Ben Carson, *The Big Picture* (Grand Rapids, Mich.: Zondervan, 1999).

2. Verna Carson, Karen L. Soeken, and Patricia M. Grimm, "Hope and Its Relationship to Spiritual Well-Being," *Journal of Psychology and Theology* 16, no. 2 (1988): 159–167.

3. Christopher G. Ellison, "Religious Involvement and Subjective Well-Being," *Journal of Health and Social Behavior* 32, no. 1 (1991): 193–202.

4. Patricia D. Roth, "Spiritual Well-Being and Marital Adjustment," *Journal of Psychology and Theology* 16, no. 2 (1988): 153–158.

5. William R. Mattox, "Aha! Call It the Revenge of the Church Ladies," *USA Today,* 11 February 1999, 15A.

6. Mattox, "Revenge of the Church Ladies."

7. Adam Davidson, "The Joy of No Sex," *Rolling Stone,* 14 October 1998: 81–82.

8. M. Baker and R. Gorsuch, "Trait Anxiety and Intrinsic-Extrinsic Religiousness," *Journal for the Scientific Study of Religion* 21 (1982): 119–22.

9. P. L. Benson and B. P. Spilka, "God-Image As a Function of Self-Esteem and Locus of Control," *Journal for the Scientific Study of Religion* 12, no. 3 (1973): 297–310.

10. H. G. Koenig et al., "Religion and Anxiety Disorder," *Journal of Anxiety Disorders* 7 (1993): 321–342.

11. G. W. Comstock and K. B. Partridge, "Church Attendance and Health," *Journal of Chronic Diseases* 25 (1972): 665–672.

12. Philip Yancey, *Soul Survivor* (New York: Galilee/Doubleday, 2001), 1.

13. C. S. Lewis, *Surprised by Joy* (New York: Harvest Book/Harcourt, Inc., 1955).

CHAPTER 9: My Family's Transformation

1. Murray Bowen, *Family Therapy in Clinical Practice* (New York: Aronson, 1978), 467–547.

APPENDIX: Test Your Family's Transformation IQ

1. M. Scott Peck, *The Road Less Traveled: A New Psychology of Love, Traditional Values and Spiritual Growth* (New York: Touchstone Books/Simon & Schuster, 1978), 98.

2. John Gottman and Nan Silver, *The Seven Principles for Making Marriage Work* (New York: Three Rivers Press, 1999), 100.

3. Susan Forward, *Emotional Blackmail* (New York: Harper Collins, 1997), 196–209.

4. Patricia Evans, *The Verbally Abusive Relationship: How to Recognize It and How to Respond* (Holbrook, Mass.: Adams Media Corporation, 1996), 60–78.